Start Here

Practical help
in solving
literacy problems
in the classroom

by

Beth Smith

NASON
PUBLISHING

First published in 1998 by
Nason Publishing,
PO Box 243,
Harpenden AL5 1ZT

Copyright © Beth Smith 1998

Beth Smith asserts her right to be
identified as author of this work,
in accordance with the Copyright,
Designs and Patents Act 1988.

Editor: Ruth Nason
Design: Carole Binding
Illustration: Lorna Wang

Printed and bound by
Stanley L. Hunt (Printers) Ltd,
Rushden, Northamptonshire

ISBN 0 9534203 0 2

A CIP catalogue record for
this book is available from
the British Library

All rights reserved. No part of this
publication may be reproduced,
stored in a retrieval system, or
transmitted in any form or by any
means, without prior permission
in writing from the publisher.

Foreword

Moved by the distress that reading and spelling problems can cause in families, I became dedicated to trying to release people into literacy.

Very soon after I started teaching I was fortunate to be sent on a special in-service training course. One day a week for a year, a small group of us learned from some of Britain's top professionals about all aspects of literacy. We were to share our newly-acquired knowledge and insight with other teachers. Over the years I have built on this foundation and have gained much further knowledge and experience from my own work. I have taught in a number of schools, helping all ages of children to overcome problems with reading, writing and spelling.

In the course of my work I have run in-service training sessions. One was specifically for experienced junior school teachers who felt that they did not know enough about the teaching of reading. I kept these sessions deliberately very practical and jargon-free, and tried to give a framework of understanding of the whole of literacy and how it all meshes together. I was struck by the unusual number of people who afterwards asked me to write a book along the same lines. It has taken some years, but here is that book.

I am deeply grateful to family and friends who have kept me at it, to all those who have given me their professional advice, in particular my close friend Jean Sergeant, and to Ruth Nason for her sensitive, intelligent editing. But I am conscious that I owe most to those teachers in my own childhood who showed me what teaching was all about.

Beth Smith

Contents

Contents

Contents

Contents

6 Reading: the general picture

7 Handwriting

Contents

Contents

Appendix

Chapter One

Please start here

Throughout the book

Throughout the book, unless a child is specifically identified as a girl, I have used the pronouns 'he' and 'him' to make the text clearer and simpler to read. The choice of pronoun was made not from sexism but because during my teaching career I have come across far more boys than girls with literacy problems.

Anecdotes are based on what actually happened, but I have changed names and certain details.

Throughout the book, I have used the verb 'to teach' to mean that learning takes place. If we set out to teach a child something but he fails to learn it, then we have not taught him – we have only tried to teach him.

The word 'need' occurs frequently in every part of the book, but you will not find me telling you what you ought, must or should do. We are all different, the children are all different, and the circumstances are all different. I can only try to clarify problems and suggest what may need to be done to solve them. I do not expect you to be able to fulfil all those needs – who can in teaching? But perhaps if I have made them clearer for you, you will be better able to assess the situation and balance priorities.

In roughly the right direction

The book is planned so that you can use it as you like. Dip into it, or find the chapter you need, or read the book from cover to cover. The detailed list of contents and the index are designed to help you locate a particular problem. Throughout the text there are references to pages in other chapters, since a child's problems in one area of literacy are often closely linked with his progress in another. For example, a beginner reader with problems may be failing to use length and shape to help him distinguish between words. We may help him best by working on his uneven handwriting, getting him to understand and achieve the correct size and position of letters relative to each other.

When suggesting possible solutions to a problem, I can only hope to point you in roughly the right direction. It may not be the best path or the most popular one, but I believe you will not go far wrong in heading out that way.

Remember common sense?

Much of the book is simple, obvious common sense but, judging from what I have seen in schools and classrooms over the years, it needs to be stated. Perhaps some teacher training courses have concentrated too much on the theoretical. I have certainly come across student teachers, mature students in particular, who felt they were having to suppress their common sense in order to become qualified. In addition, I have seen experienced teachers reluctantly stifle their common sense and professional judgement in order not to damage their careers when educational chiefs and school heads have enthusiastically taken up new trends and theories.

Support and encouragement

One of the most important things we can offer the child struggling to read, spell or achieve better handwriting is a caring, sensitive relationship, one in which he is listened to, consulted, and respected as another human being, albeit a much younger one.

Our intention may be to encourage the child, but how adept are we at doing that? To be effective, praise needs careful wording. 'Good boy!' resounds in many primary schools, but we do better to state our feelings and talk about what we see and what he has or has not done.

'I enjoyed the way you read that.'
'Wow! I see your name written clearly. All the letters are on

the line, and the *a* starts in the right place.'

'Ah, I noticed that you went on reading to see if you could get any clue about the word and then went back to it. Splendid!'

'Your desk top is clear, your books are positioned well, and you have a finger on the word you are copying. A pleasure to see.'

The child hears that he has done something right and so feels OK. But if we praise him himself and tell him that he is a good boy for getting something right, it does not ring quite true, for he knows he is no angel – who is? And what kind of boy is he when he tries very hard and does not get it right? Naughty? Wicked and totally unloved?

Are you still hanging on to 'Good boy'? Consider how you feel when people praise you. 'You're a wonderful person!' or 'You're a marvellous cook!' come across to many of us as excessive and rather insincere. We feel uncomfortable. In contrast, 'I'm delighted that you have fixed it so neatly!' or 'Mmm, delicious!' can leave us feeling appreciated and successful on this one occasion without the need to live up to an impossibly high standard.

The same goes for expressing disapproval and anger. Anger is better directed not at the child but at the situation. 'You stupid idiot!' is not helpful, nor is 'How many times have I told you ...?' A clearer, more effective message would be: 'I feel furious when I see books stuffed back carelessly. I expect you to put them back the right way up and in the right order.' Stating clearly what we are angry about and what we want done about the situation is helpful communication. We have not attacked the child himself.

In general, addressing the situation is preferable to passing judgement on the child. An 'I' statement is likely to be more helpful than a 'You' one, and questions ('What's the matter with you today?') are best avoided. 'Why?' questions are particularly apt to be seen as attacking, no matter how innocent the query was intended to be (for example, 'Why did you do that?').

Chapter 1

Who else, if not ourselves? When, if not now?

It is up to us to try to tackle a child's basic problem with literacy as best we may, here and now. The longer a child's problem remains unsolved, the more complex it becomes, the more ground the child loses and the longer it will take to put things right.

To argue that the teachers and the schools and even the parents before us 'ought to have taught that and it's too late now – we've got to get on with *our* job' is a cop-out. So is it for infant and junior schools to adopt an easy-going attitude over laying down the foundations of basic literacy, arguing that 'It will come in time. Look what we have achieved already – the exciting creative writing the children are doing, and have you seen the wonderful work they have done this term on colour?' This is of little consolation to teachers further up the line who are thrown into despair by the literacy problems that reach them.

The one who suffers most when we do not all work as a team is the person who leaves school with unnecessarily poor spelling or an unhelpful pen hold or inadequate skills for reading. We need to battle on behalf of the future adults that we are teaching now. Of course not every battle can be won. Nonetheless, this book sets out to equip you better for the fray.

Chapter Two

Comprehension

This chapter examines the sort of reading comprehension problems that we may be able to clear up in the course of ordinary classroom teaching. First we consider children who have varying degrees of difficulty in comprehending any and all texts, and we look at three major ways of helping them. Then, starting from page 27, we consider children who usually have little or no difficulty understanding what they are reading but who have specific difficulties on occasions.

Just reading mechanically

A beginner reader may read reasonably accurately but so mechanically that he might just as well be 'barking at print', like a performing dog. A dog can be trained to bark and stop barking at a signal. The audience sees the mathematical symbol for two, and the dog barks twice; but, as the symbol has no mathematical meaning for the dog, it would be just as ready to bark once or three times. In somewhat the same way, a child may 'read' mechanically, without understanding what reading is all about.

Probably we all experience times when we read mechanically, taking in little or nothing of what we are reading at that moment, and children are no different. Distracted by some temporary upset, or made to read a book that he finds facile and boring, a child may read mechanically with his mind elsewhere. However, usually a child knows what it is to understand fully what he is reading, whereas the children we are considering in this section appear not to have reached that understanding.

Gavin (see page 19) was reading fluently and accurately and, until I interrupted him to discuss what he had read,

I had no inkling of how mechanically he was reading. I found that, up to then, reading had been just something he 'did', line by line and page by page. The meaning of what he read did not impinge on his inner thoughts and feelings. He saw reading just in terms of 'getting on'.

A very sorry picture

Some beginner readers present a much sorrier picture than Gavin did. A child may read a story word by word as if reading a list of sight words, or perhaps he sounds out every single word so laboriously that he forgets what the previous word was, let alone the rest of the sentence and the passage. Either way, if he misreads a word he will probably not correct it, and may start and stop anywhere, regardless of full stops and meaning. He may not seem to notice, let alone mind, that he has read nonsense.

What we can do to help

How do we set about helping a child with such difficulties? There seem to be some obvious courses of action. For example, if the child appears to be treating every word as a sight word, we encourage him to use contextual cues and we try to build up his phonic skills. If the child sounds out each word, we can encourage him to use clues from context to help guess the word, and we can also try to build up the number of words that he recognises by sight. We encourage all beginner readers to look through a story and its pictures before reading it, so that they may gain some idea of what it is likely to be about. Our whole approach to reading will contain a strong emphasis on meaning.

However sensible and straightforward these remedial efforts are, they may not be enough to help. There may well be an underlying emotional cause for a child having problems over comprehending what he is reading. Severe difficulties in general comprehension are beyond the scope of this book, and it is assumed that a child exhibiting such difficulties will already have been referred to a psychologist or other appropriate professional for assessment and help.

> *Gavin, aged seven, read aloud to me, 'All children like reading.'*
>
> *I asked him if he agreed.*
>
> *'What do you mean?' he asked, looking at me blankly.*
>
> *'Read that bit again, and then tell me if you think that's true.'*
>
> *Looking mystified, he read it aloud again, and started on the next line.*
>
> *'Wait a minute, Gavin. You've just read that all children like reading. Do you think that is true? Do all children like reading?'*
>
> *'Yes,' said Gavin.*
>
> *'Everybody likes reading? Including you?'*
>
> *'Yes', said Gavin, and then, impatiently, 'Can I get on now?'*
>
> *'But I thought you said this morning that you didn't like reading.'*
>
> *'I HATE it.'*

If that is the case, we may have been able to get specific advice about how we can help the child in the classroom. In the absence of such professional guidance, we help the child as best we can.

I make three major suggestions for helping a beginner reader who has an overall problem in fully comprehending what he reads:

- use the Context Game (see Chapter 4, page 61);
- use the Action Game (see this chapter, page 22);
- use his personal dictation to form one of his reading books (see pages 20-22).

If a child's reading comprehension does not improve considerably after a short time of such varied activities, consider getting him referred to an educational psychologist if this has not already been put in hand.

Using the child's own dictation

Not just for five-year-olds

The practice of getting a child to draw a picture and then dictate what word or words he wants written down to accompany it is widespread in lower infant classes, but it may also help some older children who have reading problems. It is certainly worth trying with a beginner reader who has serious problems with comprehension.

If, very unusually, the child we want to help has never, or hardly ever, drawn and dictated like this in the past, we now give him plenty of opportunity to do so.

● Get him to draw a picture. Take down what he would like to say in connection with it. (Note that most young children not only prefer to draw their picture before dictating, but find it necessary to do so. It is only when they are older and more mature that they find it easy to write first and then draw.)

● Write or print out in large letters one or more good sentences derived from his words. Read them to him and with him, until he can read them by himself. Make sure that he can point to each word as he says it, in case he has merely learnt each sentence off by heart without matching it to the words on the page.

● Make a collection of the child's pictures and sentences and use it as his personal reading book to be kept safely and read frequently in addition to his ordinary reading book.

- Reading and writing are closely linked at this stage, so write or print out each sentence again in large letters, to be used as work sheets. Make sure that the child can read these sentences now he has no pictures to prompt him. Then get him to trace over the words or to copy them underneath, preferably more than once, so that he begins to learn to write and spell these words that are personal to him.

So much for the child who has done little or nothing of this sort of thing before. But what of the child who has done much of it already in previous classes? How is it that he has still not grasped that reading is meaningful? Without the answer to that one, I can only suggest that we try again as described, and see how it goes.

Meaningful dictation

We would like the child to dictate something that is going to be really meaningful to him when he sees it written. Faced with an inarticulate or indecisive child, we may be tempted to rush in with 'helpful' suggestions of what we think he would like written – and miss the mark. We need to try to stand back, relax, and let him find his own words. That will be easier for him if he feels safe and not badgered or crowded.

What if the child cannot think of anything to dictate after he has drawn his picture, and will not even discuss his picture with us? We can suggest that he might like us to write 'I can't think of anything to say about this picture' or 'I don't want to say anything about this picture'. I have found that these two suggestions can be a way in. The child either accepts one with a laugh, and laughs again whenever he reads it, or will suddenly straighten up, protest, 'Oh, but I *want* to say something!', and start dictating with decision. If we give him freedom like this, what he eventually dictates may have a deep personal meaning for him. We need to respect this. He does not have to explain.

If he cannot think what to draw in the first place, we may need to reassure him that that is OK with us and that he can take his time. Anxiety can block. Is he worried about making a mistake? We tell him that he can take more paper if necessary. This permission does not usually lead, in my experience, to a crumpled sheet, let alone a full waste bin. On the contrary, it tends to help the child to relax and allow his creativity to surface.

If after some time he is still stuck, we suggest he draws one line on the paper, any old line, to see if that gets him going. Or how does he feel about having the words 'I can't think of anything to draw today' written at the bottom of the blank sheet of paper?

We keep all these drawings and dictations safely, preferably gathered into a book. We read the words with the child until he knows them, and then we encourage him to read them to himself and to us on numerous occasions. This may be helpful to him long after he has moved ahead with his reading and writing.

If he is reluctant to use a book like this, feeling that it is babyish, we can suggest that he copies the words (correctly) onto the computer and prints them out. Then he can stick them and his original pictures onto sheets of paper to form a book with an impressive layout.

The Action Game

Outline of the game

The Action Game is a simple game of carrying out written commands. We need a number of pieces of card on each of which is written in large, clear print a single word like 'hop' or 'clap'. We show a word. The child has to read it silently and do the action. The child can be on his own or in a group. Words to use with beginner readers are suggested opposite. Harder and longer commands can be used with better readers.

Suggested words for the Action Game

1. The choice of commands will depend on what
    sight words the child is likely to know and what
    phonics, if any. All the following words can be
    read if the child knows his single letter sounds
    and can blend them. (See Appendix, page 155, for
    single letter sounds, and page 54 for blending.)

    run, sit, jump, sob, clap, nod, hop, wink, blink.
    (Touch your:) leg, neck, back, hand, ribs, hip.
    (Touch something:) big, soft, red, wet.
    (Pretend to be:) a cat, a dog, a pig, hot.

2. All the following commands use a family of
    words such as parts of the body. The child may
    know some of these common words already by
    sight, and may be able to guess most of the
    others in the same family if he uses what
    phonics he can muster, including **sh**, **ch** and **th**.

    (Show me your:) leg, hand, head, hair, neck,
    chin, chest, ankle, foot, toe, finger, nose,
    shoulder, fist, thumb, shin, eye, ear, knee, wrist.

    (Point to the:) door, chair, table, window,
    carpet, wall, television, computer, gerbil.

    (Show me:) a pencil, a book, a shoe, a coat,
    a hat, a lunch box.

    (Touch something:) red, blue, yellow, green,
    orange, white, black, pink, purple, brown.

    (Touch something:) soft, hard, big, small, hot,
    cold, smooth, rough.

Chapter 2

Explaining the game

We explain carefully to the child that he is to read the word inside his head and then do the action. To begin with, he will probably just read the word aloud. He may need quite a bit of convincing that that is not sufficient. 'Yes, that's the right word, but now you have to *do* something.' For him this may take an enormous leap in comprehension, and so, when he matches the action with the word for the first time, he deserves an enthusiastic response from us.

Achieving our purpose

Once he has the idea of taking action, it is essential to leave him to decide for himself what the next words are. We need to resist his attempts to get praise or reassurance at the reading stage. We have to hold off until he does the action. It is not the reading of the word but the meaningful response to it that is going to get our attention and approval. In the past he has been getting the latter for just saying the word, for just barking at print. We are now trying to teach him that what we are really expecting him to do is to work out what that print means.

For example, if he tries, '*Hop*. It says *hop*, Miss. That's right, isn't it?', we reply with a sympathetic smile, 'Well, is it or isn't it? I'm not telling you. I'm waiting for you to *do* something.'

What if he still asks each time? Here we are into a deeper level of teaching. Is he a child who has learned that his Mum always gives in if he goes on long enough? A silent grin from us will show him he is not going to win. He will probably grin back and get on with it. Is he, on the other hand, desperate for reassurance? We acknowledge his feelings and quietly expect him to carry on. 'It can be scary not knowing whether you are right or not. However, come on. Have a go. If you are wrong, you can always try again.'

Reading silently

We emphasise that he is to read the words silently. We do not need to hear him. We will know by his actions whether he is right or not, and our long-term aim is to encourage silent, independent reading. However, someone at this early stage of reading may need to mouth the word or say it to himself very quietly to help himself read it. Indeed, it may be the first time that he has tried reading silently (see page 85).

Playing the Action Game with a group

When playing the game with a group, we can start by showing a card and asking all the children to do the action. Once they have got the idea we can carry on like that or ask individual children. The latter gives us the opportunity to pick easy words for beginner readers, and to provide harder words or sentences for better readers.

When a group of children play the game, silent reading is particularly important. We need to be constantly on the alert for children who only appear to be doing what we have asked them to do. In this game we want all the children to have the experience of reading words and acting on them (read, understand, act). If one child works out the word aloud, others, hearing him, may do the action before he does. Some of them may have read the word for themselves silently and have been going to do the action anyway, but others could be merely reacting to what they heard (hear, understand, act), which was not the point of the lesson. Furthermore, the child himself who was sounding out aloud may still be just barking at print. He has worked out the word, but may then just be copying the action of the other children (read, no action, look, copy the action).

Occasional individual turns will reveal any child who still has not got the idea or who cannot read the words for some reason.

Difficulties

What if a child does the wrong action or apparently cannot read the word at all?

Sight words If a child has been taught no phonics, and the words he knows are mainly only those in his reading book, most of the commands I have suggested may be beyond him to read. Did he manage to read and respond to hardly more than the common colours (e.g. 'Touch something blue')? He needs a wider sight recognition vocabulary and to be introduced to phonics so that he can at least begin to use the sound of the initial letter or letters in a word (see Chapter 5, Sight words, and Chapter 3, Phonics.)

Phonics What phonic skills is he using, if any?

● Does he not know all the single letter sounds? Could he not even identify the initial sound of the word? (See Chapter 3, Phonics, variously, pages 45-53.)

● If he managed the initial sound but muddled 'leg' and 'lip', for example, is the trouble that he cannot sound out words? (See Phonics, page 54, 'Difficulties with sounding out and blending'.)

● If he knows his letter sounds, and can blend and sound out, does he use this knowledge to help him read words? Is he perhaps just looking at the word, trying to remember if he has seen it before, or just watching the other children for clues? (See Phonics, page 57, 'The child who avoids sounding out', and pages 55-56 for a child who is not learning.)

Letters Is he having trouble identifying letters?

● Is he confusing *d* with *b* or *p*, or *m* with *w*, for example? (See page 70, 'Getting letters and words the wrong way round'.)

● Have we used the printed form of *a* (a) or *g* (g) which he has not met before?

● Is he used only to infant print while we have used cursive loops which are confusing him? Or are we expecting him to read our definitely idiosyncratic handwriting? (Have you noticed how savage and venomous some colleagues can get if there is any suggestion that their handwriting is a problem to a child? It is a remarkably sensitive area. 'Well, he *ought* to be able to read it, and if he can't, that's his bad luck.' Some very poor readers in junior and senior schools have an awful lot of bad luck.)

Other reasons What about the checklist we need to keep at the back of our minds all the time?

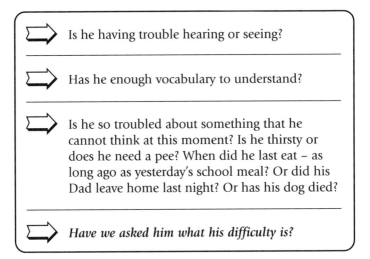

> Is he having trouble hearing or seeing?

> Has he enough vocabulary to understand?

> Is he so troubled about something that he cannot think at this moment? Is he thirsty or does he need a pee? When did he last eat – as long ago as yesterday's school meal? Or did his Dad leave home last night? Or has his dog died?

> *Have we asked him what his difficulty is?*

Comprehension problems met by better readers

We now consider times when a child may have difficulty in reading comprehension even though that is normally not a problem. Please note, however, that we are not going to consider the child who is failing to understand mainly because of lack of intelligence, poor language development, inadequate general knowledge and experience, etc. Such problems are beyond the scope of this book. So are those caused by emotional factors. If we have taken into account all other factors, including the points raised in the rest of this section, and we still see no reason why a particular child should be so lacking in comprehension, can we get him assessed properly through the school services?

Chapter 2

Failing to correct obvious mistakes when reading

Consider the child who often misreads or omits important words, or skips a whole line, or reads straight over full stops and paragraphs, so that the result is nonsense. Does he just carry on regardless if we do not intervene? If so, he is clearly not comprehending what he is reading.

Are the words too hard? Context does not always help to identify a word, and if the child has difficulty with too many words in a passage, words that he cannot work out ('gaol') or has never heard of before ('rite'), he will have lost sight of the context anyway. He is not likely to be able to read effectively on his own if he encounters more than four or five difficult words in a hundred.

Is the language too hard? When he meets unfamiliar phrases and turns of English, he is more likely to misread even common words he knows well, because he expects something else. Take the construction 'Little did he realise that ...'. A child who has never met it before is likely to expect a noun rather than a verb after 'little'. I overheard one child misreading it as 'Little dogs have real ...'. He hesitated, got the next word ('that') correct, and then hesitated again before reading on. He was clearly confused but carried on presumably because he had given up hoping to understand what he was reading.

Poor child. This is not what reading is all about. He needs to read something easier, or to have someone by his side explaining and helping him through the difficult bits by reading to him or with him. The only possible justification for getting him to struggle on so miserably by himself is that he is on the last part of a standard reading test.

Difficulty answering comprehension questions

Does the child sometimes find it difficult to understand the comprehension question itself, let alone to find the answer,

One 13-year-old boy, understanding practically nothing of German, nevertheless obtained 43 per cent in an end-of-year language exam. He did this by noting what unfamiliar words were contained in the question, looking for those words in the given German passage, and copying down the sentence in which he found them.

despite the fact that his reading is generally no problem? Suggest that he tries reading the question aloud, or mouthing it under his breath. This adds hearing and the movements of his speech muscles to sight, helping to pin his mind to the task. Once may not be enough. However hard we try to concentrate, we may have to repeat a question in this fashion several times before it begins to make sense.

Given that he has managed to understand the question, has he bothered to read the original passage? Obviously he needs to, but perhaps he avoids what he regards as hard work and instead just searches through the text vaguely looking for a key word. Or is it that he has read the text but has retained little of it? We can all do that on occasions. His mind has been on other things, his own personal affairs, distractions in the classroom, or even worries that he is not going to understand the passage. Suggest that he rereads the passage slowly, mouthing it as explained above, and repeating a phrase or a sentence as necessary until he gets 'into' what he is reading.

Is he searching systematically enough to find the answer, or is he instead looking vaguely and then giving up with the usual assertion that 'It doesn't say'? We can show him how we might set about searching. We explain that there are no set rules, and that we may search in different ways depending on what we are looking for.

I offer the following as an example, but certainly no model, of how we can share our own methods with the child. In this instance it amounts to having a guess, then widening the search using scanning, and then intensifying the search. Even encouraging the child to use his finger to direct his eyes may help him considerably.

I might say to the child: 'When I meet a question like this, I go about it this way. I try to remember where the answer might be, and I look there first. Let's see ... No, I can't find it there.

'I now quickly scan the whole piece. The question is about the stranger's violin, so I am specially looking for the word "violin" ... No, no luck.

'If I am still stuck, then what I do is start at the beginning, even though I don't think the answer is going to be there. It just might be. *I put my finger on the words like this*, to help me concentrate, and I read carefully right through until I find the bit about the violin. Ah, here we are!'

'But it doesn't say, Miss!'

Another common problem over comprehension questions arises when the answer is only obtained by reasoning. A child may be flummoxed if he has been used to finding the answer directly expressed in words and is now, without warning, faced with a question that requires him to understand what is only implied. It is hardly surprising if he indignantly protests, 'It does not say!'

Some children have no further difficulty once we have explained that they must work out the answer. Others may need us to go through several examples with them before they are confident enough to deduce an answer themselves.

Be alert when marking printed comprehension questions wrong. Occasionally the obvious answer, the one printed in the book, is not the only possible one. Suppose the text says that Sharon helps her mother feed and dress Melanie, and the question is: Who is the older, Sharon or Melanie? The expected answer is Sharon, but a particular child living with a severely disabled older sibling at home may decide that it

is Melanie, or make the usual complaint, 'It doesn't say, Miss!'
This leads to the consideration of possibility and probability.

'But I've looked, and it still doesn't say, Miss!'

Some years ago I used a comprehension exercise which states
that the snow has just gone, the birds are singing and
gathering grass, wool and straw to make their nests, and the
daffodils are out. The questions are: What time of year is it,
summer, autumn or spring? Are these birds in the town or in
the country?

Jasmine complained, with good reason, that she could not
find the first answer. It turned out that she had no idea which
season of the year was associated with daffodils and nest-
building, and, indeed, was very hazy about the seasons in
general. A child lacking background knowledge cannot be
expected to understand fully a passage like this.

Cameron, on the other hand, also said: 'It does not say.
You can't tell the answer to either of them.' When questioned
about the seasons, he said: 'Well, it might be Australia.' The
answer would still have been spring, but his objection
showed his refusal to commit himself when faced with
uncertainty. This intelligent 12-year-old was doing this
exercise because he had become aware that he often did
not pick up the gist of what he was reading or of what people
were talking about, and did not know why he was having
this trouble.

Cameron and I looked at the exercise closely and
discussed possibilities and probabilities. The birds were
probably in the country, but not necessarily so, since grass,
wool and straw could all conceivably be found in the town,
and, yes, it might be Australia or New Zealand. We could not
tell from the amount of information provided so far, but
could make only an intelligent guess at the most probable
answer while keeping other possibilities in mind. We could
revise or confirm the guess if and when other information
became available.

We then talked briefly about inferences and assumptions
in conversations, and I gave him some examples of how

people clarify, and of how we all occasionally get the wrong end of the stick. This discussion helped Cameron considerably. He began to give full rein to his quick mind.

Tailpiece

The following account was written from memory immediately after taking a group of four 11-year-old boys for the last fifteen minutes on a Friday afternoon. Names have been changed, as they have been throughout this book.

Asked to take these boys at a moment's notice, I seized the nearest thing to hand, by chance the book of exercises mentioned on the previous page (A. G. Roberts, *Book 1*, *Reading and Thinking*, Learning Materials Ltd, Wolverhampton).

I read out the following question in a dull voice:

> *A man was going down the garden. He was carrying a*
> *spade. He took his coat off. What was he going to do?*
> *a) climb a tree?*
> *b) dig a hole?*
> *c) go for a ride?*
> *Was the weather warm?*

The boys gave me answers that seemed obvious to them, that he was going to dig a hole, and that the weather was warm. I said 'Yes' and repeated their answers, as dully. I added that they could be right, and that it was the sort of answer they expected to give at school.

Then I said with energy: 'Prove to me that the *real* answer is that he is going for a ride.'

Terry got the idea straightaway. He said: 'The man's going to put his spade away in the shed, get his bike out and go for a ride.'

I said: 'Oh, well done, a better idea than the one I had thought of!'

Darryl said: 'He might have borrowed the spade and put it in the back of his car to take it back.'

'Great!' I said, and added – wanting to show them how

they could vary it, 'or maybe he's taking the spade over to his grandmother to dig her garden for her because she can't manage it.'

I left it there, the other two boys, Sam and Carl, not having spoken. I then asked the four of them to prove that he was really going to climb the tree.

Darryl had a go this time. 'He's clearing the ground of all the twigs before he climbs the tree.'

Terry and Carl elaborated on this theme – branches and leaves were suggested.

'What if he takes the spade with him when he climbs the tree?' I asked.

Darryl, still on the idea of clearing up twigs: 'He's using the spade to chop the branches down.'

'Yes,' I said, noticing they were still rather restricted, 'or perhaps he's trying to rescue the new kitten they've just got, and as the kitten won't get down he's prodding it with the spade.'

Variations on this were then offered.

'Why did he take his coat off?' I asked.

'Because it was warm.'

'Another reason?'

Carl immediately said: 'He's got a very new smart leather coat and he doesn't want to spoil it.'

Terry nodded eagerly: 'Black, with tassels.'

Again I joined in deliberately: 'Mmm, I like that. But what if he's got a nagging wife who says "It's no use you expecting me to sew on any more buttons if they get ripped off on that tree. I've told you before ..."?'

Unexpected grins.

'What if he really is going to dig a hole? Can you think of an interesting reason?'

I was surprised at how ordinary their replies were: he was planting some things, he was weeding, etc.

'An *interesting* reason?' I asked again.

Carl said he had bought some manure and was going to put it in the hole, and it was all smelly and squelchy. This was greeted with exclamations and mild sniggers.

I intervened again: 'What if it was a really *deep* hole? What might he be digging that for?'

Darryl's face lit up. 'TREASURE!' he said quietly but with great satisfaction.

Terry started saying: 'He might be digging a tunnel ...'

Sam quickly added: 'To escape his nagging wife,' and burst out laughing. This was the first time he had spoken.

Carl had been very quiet and suddenly suggested: 'He's digging his grave.'

I thought, phew, what is going on with you, my lad?, and varied it again: 'Or he's going to bury his nagging wife.'

Terry said: 'He's burying his cat.'

Sam: 'He was up the tree and dropped the spade on it accidentally.'

'The next door neighbour's cat,' said Darryl.

'A dog,' said Carl.

I said we would have to stop there as it was the end of school that day. 'So if you have got some very dull, boring work to do, you've got to put down the right answers, of course, but you can make it much more exciting in your head.'

They all thanked me warmly, Carl coming back into the room to do so, and I could hear them still discussing possibilities animatedly as they went along the corridor.

With hindsight there are things I would have done differently. Nevertheless, I wish all lessons went like that.

Chapter Three

Phonics

Let's be clear about phonics

Before we consider particular problems that children can have with phonics, let us look at phonics in general and how to use it to best advantage.

Phonic generalisations

Phonics is not a science like phonetics. Phonetics is the study of speech processes and uses an exact system of sound classification in which one particular printed symbol indicates one particular sound. Phonics is just a method of teaching people to read by remembering the sounds that letters are likely to indicate, and it is certainly not precise. It could not be, because there are only the 26 letters of the alphabet to indicate more than 40 different sounds in spoken English. Not only that, but some sounds are indicated in more than one way. That gives us a formidable number of phonic generalisations, some overlapping. You will find a list of the main ones in the Appendix, page 155.

The need to have a sight recognition vocabulary

There are numerous exceptions to these 'rules' and, unluckily for beginner readers, the greatest proportion of these exceptions are found amongst the most frequently occurring words in early reading, words like *one* ('wun') and *who* ('hoo'). We meet more and more regular words as our reading progresses, but we still have to cope with the quirky ones, including the infamous 'ough' group. 'Ough' is pronounced differently in each of the following eight words: rough, cough, bough, hough, though, thought, through, thorough.

Chapter 3

Beginner readers need to build up a stock of words that they can recognise by sight. Even if we teach a child phonics, he still needs this 'sight vocabulary'. If he does not know the common irregular words, he will be confined to sentences like 'Ben had a pet pig' and 'Meg is in a red van'. There are also all the phonically regular words that he will come across long before he has sufficient phonics to analyse them, words such as 'birthday' and 'school'. (See Chapter 5, Sight words.)

Using context, grammar and shape to help

Working out word after word by phonics alone can be heavy work for a child. He will find it much easier and quicker to identify words if he meets them in ordinary reading and uses his phonic knowledge together with all the cues that he can get from context and grammar and from the length and shape of words. With these cues to help, he may often need only a pinch of phonics before making an intelligent guess. Suppose, for example, in a simple book about jungle rivers, he comes across the words 'Look out! There is a ...'. The next word is long and starts with 'cro'. He would do best to guess at 'crocodile' at this point rather than to sound out the whole word. If his guess does not make sense as he goes on reading, he can always go back and look at the word more thoroughly. (See Chapter 4, Context, grammar and punctuation. Also see page 81, 'Shape'; and pages 54-59, 'Difficulties with sounding out and blending'.)

If phonics is used flexibly, not on its own but combined with other reading strategies, it becomes a strong part of reading attack skills and a lifebelt for weak readers struggling without it.

Of course we want the child to be able to work out a whole word, syllable by syllable, if necessary. But getting him to sound out endless lists of phonic words and/or insisting that he spends time working out a long word which is not crucial to understanding the exciting part of the story are not perhaps the best ways to encourage him. So, what about improving his ability to sound out and read long words through developing his spelling and copying skills? Good spelling and copying involve analysis of words, awareness of syllables, and of how letters in a written word usually correspond with the sound of the word. (See page 115, 'Not analysing the word?', and Chapter 9, Spelling and dictation, variously, pages 132, 143 and 148.)

Irregular words

As the child progresses to harder reading material and his phonic skills improve, the irregular new words that he comes across will, with luck, yield to the type of intelligent guesswork just described. There are words, though, that he will have little chance of working out from phonics and context – wildly irregular words that he has never even heard of. He is likely to be defeated by words like 'chassis', 'quay' and 'aborigine'. We ourselves may be beaten by 'Chihuahua' if we have never heard of this Mexican city or breed of tiny dog (roughly pronounced 'chi-wah-wah'), or by 'ceilidh', an informal social gathering in Scotland or Ireland with music and dancing (pronounced 'KAY-lih').

If we cannot make sense of the word, what do we do then? There is nothing for it but to ask someone, or look the word up in a dictionary, or risk mispronouncing and misunderstanding it. Once we have found out what the word is, we need to memorise it so that we can recognise it in future. (We can use phonics sometimes to help to remember the oddest spellings. See pages 68, 116 and 126.)

How much phonic knowledge do we ourselves need?

Some of us learned to read without the help of phonics, but if we are involved in the teaching of literacy at any level we need to know about it. Whether we are introducing the sounds of the alphabet to five-year-olds or trying to improve the spelling of teenagers, a thorough grasp of phonics will broaden our understanding of how to avoid and overcome reading and spelling problems. Putting it another way, we need to be able to see and appreciate the whole wood, even though in the classroom we may be occupied in pointing out only a few trees or branches.

Chapter 3

Phonics beyond the alphabet

Introducing sh, th, ch

When we introduce children to phonics, the obvious place to start is with the letters of the alphabet. (See Appendix, page 155, for a list of their sounds and a guide to pronouncing them as helpfully as possible.) Note that the vowel sounds of the alphabet are all short (*a*, apple; *e*, elephant; *i*, igloo; *o*, orange; *u*, umbrella). We can teach the children to read short words in the form consonant-short vowel-consonant (as in 'man' and 'leg'). However, I do not consider this first stage complete until we have also taught the sounds of **sh**, **th** and **ch**. What about adding them (with appropriate pictures) to the end of a phonic alphabet on the wall?

Why do I think this important? It is not just because those extra sounds open up so many new words, but because learning them helps a child to grasp that there is more to phonics than just the alphabet. We want him to realise that not only single letters but groups of letters may correspond with the sounds of spoken English. If he had originally got the idea that letter sounds were just alternative 'names' for letters, he may now have a rethink. (See page 43.)

Groups of two letters representing one sound are called digraphs. **Sh**, **th** and **ch** are consonant digraphs. Does the child now recognise these three digraphs and remember their sounds? Can he now read a variety of words made up of a short vowel in the middle and a consonant or consonant digraph at each end (as in 'shop' and 'fish')? He may now be ready to move on from short single vowel sounds and learn other digraphs such as **ay** (as in 'day'), **oa** (as in 'boat') and **ir** (as in 'first'). However, how is he getting on with consonant clusters?

Difficulties over consonant clusters

Some children, once they know the alphabet sounds, have no difficulty with consonant clusters (sometimes called consonant blends). Other children may need a great deal of practice before they move from single consonants to being able to tackle *st-* or *-mp*, for example. There are over 40 initial and final consonant clusters, and these are listed in the Appendix, page 158. If a school decides that these are to be taught with a vowel, the number increases fivefold to around 200 (e.g. *bla-*, *ble-*, *bli-*, *blo-*, *blu-*). My mind boggles at the thought of any teacher conscientiously trying to drill the children thoroughly in all 200. Children learn to read in many ways. There is no need to make such heavy weather of it for them. Here are some suggestions:

● Check that you and the children are saying the sounds of consonants in the most helpful way. (See page 156 of the Appendix, and also pages 40-41 and 56.)

● When the children are sounding out a word, encourage them to emphasise the initial consonant cluster with or without the following vowel. (For example, 'CLI-ck' or 'CL-i-ck'.)

● Practising long lists of words with the same consonant cluster does not help all children. Try also introducing the words in simple sentences so the children can gain confidence by using context to help.

● Extending the above suggestion, see if you can use the Context Game (see page 61) to give the children practice in identifying initial consonant clusters. When reading the story, sound out the beginning of suitable words and ask for guesses. Emphasise the initial sound of the consonant cluster. For example: 'At last he came to the river. He forgot that the old woman had warned him not to DUH-rrr-i...' (drink). You might find an old phonic reading book very suitable for this. They are sometimes to be found in charity shops and jumble sales.

Chapter 3

What to teach next

Once the children are familiar with the sounds of the alphabet, consonant clusters and consonant digraphs, the order in which we introduce more phonics is not crucial and is often dictated more by the choice of reading material or school television programmes than by the school. Examples of magic *e* or marker *e* (see 'final *e*', Appendix pages 159-160) occur so frequently that some schools like to teach this phonic 'rule' very early on. Others consider it is so difficult to teach that they leave it until much later.

The school may have an agreed order for introducing phonic groups, but that does not mean that we cannot help and reassure a child by pointing out something in phonics long before we are likely to teach it formally. For example, although *au* occurs in a large number of long scientific words, it appears in only a very few common words (like 'August' and 'autumn'), so will not be high on any list. However, Paul is entitled to know very early on about his special *au* sound, just as Philip needs to know about his special *ph* sound and as Sean needs to know that his name is spelt in an unusual way. It is a matter of being selective and flexible.

Problems with phonics from the start

Auditory, visual and speech problems

The essential pre-reading groundwork that goes on in infant schools, particularly work on auditory and visual discrimination, is mainly beyond the scope of this book. So are the difficulties encountered by children with a visual, hearing or speech impairment. It is important to seek specialist advice about these children's individual needs and the best methods of teaching them within the class. However, there are general things that we can do to improve matters in the classroom.

When teaching phonics, aim for as little background noise as possible. Ideally, phonics should be taught in a very quiet room. But even if we achieve relative quiet in the classroom, what about sounds from outside? Music practice in the hall, workmen and traffic all conspire against us. Pick your time for phonics with this in mind.

Face the class, and articulate clearly, moving your lips. The children need to be looking at you. It is no good trying to teach phonics while half the class have their backs turned. A child with any hearing or speech difficulties or whose pronunciation is poor needs to be in a good position in the front.

Does a child seem to be mishearing or mispronouncing a letter sound? Can he repeat it accurately after you say it close to his ear, or after you tell him to watch your lips as you say the sound again?

Is a child not distinguishing between *th*, *f* and *v*? When you get a spare minute, stand or sit in front of a mirror with the child, and say the sounds. *F* is voiceless, *V* is voiced, and they are both said with the teeth slightly biting the bottom lip. The child should be able to feel his lip vibrating slightly as he voices *V*. *Th* is both voiceless (as in 'thin') and voiced (as in 'then'). When the child says either, he should be able to see the tip of his tongue in the mirror or to be able to feel it if he puts his finger against his teeth.

Remember that, even though a child has passed a hearing test recently, a heavy cold or catarrh can make it difficult temporarily for him to distinguish between certain letter sounds. If he is hardly ever without a cold or catarrh, this can badly affect his progress with reading.

Not understanding rhyme

Does a child not understand rhyme? He needs to. He has missed all the fun of playing with the sound of words that some babies and children enjoy enormously. Not only that, but he now needs to notice rhyme and rhythm to help him read words and spell them. For example, a child who can hear the link between 'west', 'best', 'nest' and 'chest' is better able to make a similar link between the words when he meets them on paper, and a child who enjoys chanting nursery rhymes or limericks rhythmically is halfway to using syllables in spelling.

Chapter 3

So what do we do to bring rhyme and rhythm into a child's life?

● Let him listen to a wide selection of rhyming poetry and verse, read by someone who clearly enjoys the rhymes and rhythm and can emphasise them.

● Let him hear a favourite poem so many times that he begins to guess what the next rhyming word will be.

● Encourage him to learn a poem or even just a rhyming couplet by heart so that he can repeat it easily. Memorising and articulating rhyming verse may help him to understand better what he has only seen and heard before.

● Play a rhyming game with a group or with this child on his own. Put out a selection of small objects such as those listed on page 48. Say a word, and the child or children have to find the object whose name rhymes with it.

● Is the child still having great difficulty identifying rhymes? Simplify the task. Rhyming is about sound, not spelling or meaning, so tell the child just to listen, perhaps with his eyes shut. Use pairs of nonsense words: 'Hotch and potch rhyme. Listen, hotch-potch. Now, do these two rhyme – hotch-lotch? Yes, they do. Now, do these two rhyme – hotch-kuzz? No. Hotch-kotch would rhyme, but not hotch-kuzz. What about hotch-quotch? Yes.' etc.

The traditional story 'Chicken Licken' contains many rhyming pairs, such as Henny Penny, Cocky Locky and Ducky Lucky, and can lead to considering other pairs such as Hong Kong, silly Billy, hurly burly, hocus pocus, higgledy piggledy, hugger-mugger. Encourage children to invent rhyming names of imaginary animals, plants and inventions, and to draw pictures of them. Let them invent rhymes for their first name or their surname, but make sure that everyone finishes up with a pleasant-sounding rhyme, or better still a complimentary one, however little deserved.

Not understanding the words used for phonics

It is not safe to assume that a child of even seven, a native English speaker, understands exactly what we mean by the words we use for phonics such as 'letter', 'word' and 'sound'. He may still have only a vague idea of what these words mean, and that idea may be inaccurate.

And what about a command like 'Listen!'? Does he understand about listening actively, or does he appear to think that 'Listen!' means just 'Stop talking!'? What seems blindingly obvious to us may not be to someone with very different life experiences – perhaps accustomed to switching off at home where 'Listen to me when I'm talking to you' is the prelude to yet another unbearable verbal battering. Or perhaps he is not accustomed to listening at all in a home where television, radio and stereo compete with each other all day.

We need to be aware of these areas of potential misunderstanding.

Not understanding what phonics is all about

I do not know how some children can experience a year or more of a complete phonic system or phonic reading scheme and work through many phonic work sheets, and yet emerge totally unaware of what phonics is all about, but I have come across them in various schools. For them letter sounds, if they know them at all, seem to be merely an alternative set of names for letters, and the Wicked Witch just a funny character who crops up with the letter **W** for some unknown reason.

If a child of seven or so has made excellent progress in reading and spelling without, apparently, understanding phonics, then fine. People learn in different ways, and he has worked out his own strategies. But keep an eye on his progress. A beginner reader who relies mainly on a very good visual memory may have need of phonics when he encounters a wider range of reading material containing an ever-increasing number of new words.

Of course, if a child of any age is lagging behind in reading and spelling, and appears not to understand phonics, that is a different matter. If we now manage to teach him what phonics is all about, that may be the vital help he needs to make good progress. Phonics has come back recently into fashion – indeed has almost been rediscovered like the wheel. I have always regarded phonics as very useful, but it is not a panacea for all ills. There may also be other help we can give a child which he needs as much as, or more than, phonics. We need to find out exactly where the child is.

- Can he play I Spy? In other words, can he identify initial sounds, at least? If he cannot, teach him. (See page 47.)

- If he can play I Spy, can he also do so if you just *show* a letter rather than making its sound? Try him with several different letters. 'I spy with my little eye something beginning with the sound of this letter.' In other words, does he know his letter sounds? We are not asking him to *tell* us the sounds, but getting him to *show* if he can use any of them in practice – two different things. If he cannot do this, can someone, adult or child, help him understand a phonic alphabet book that has several pictures to each letter? (See page 51.)

- If you show him some words in reasonably large print and sound out each one for him (moving your finger along the word), can he guess the words? If not, help him with blending. (See page 54.)

- See if you can get him to mouth short phonic words (for example, 'leg', 'hot') to himself as he copies them down. He may usually *spell* such words out as he writes them ('ell-ee-jee'). Explain that there is nothing wrong with doing that, but that you would like him now to try *saying* each word very slowly so that he starts and finishes at the same time as his writing. (If he adamantly refuses to mouth a word or say it aloud as he writes it or immediately afterwards, and leaves you feeling at other times, too, that you are getting nowhere with him, suspect emotional factors in his problem.)

- Watch him as he copies a word or a sentence or two. Can you improve his skills so that he learns usefully through copying? (See Chapter 8, which starts on page 111.)

- Does he have very poor, uneven handwriting? See if you can improve it. It would help him to make a better visual link between what he reads and what he writes. (See pages 80, 81 and 102-109.)

- Might he have eyesight or hearing difficulties that you have not been told about or that have not yet been diagnosed? If you have any suspicions, pursue the matter.

- Does he just need a general helping hand to get him going with reading – someone to read to him and with him before he reads himself? (See page 79, 'What help would the child like?') Or would peer-tutoring be the answer? (See page 90.)

If he continues to underachieve significantly, seek further advice and specialist help.

Muddling letter sounds and letter names

Some schools teach letter names first, some start with letter sounds, and still others introduce both at the same time. Be that as it may, if a child has a reading or spelling problem, then, in my opinion, it is essential that we use both name and sound and that we make a clear distinction between them.

'This is an *s* (ess). It shows a "sss" sound like the beginning of "sausage" and "snake"'.

The child can get very muddled if we talk about the sound of a letter as if it were the name of the letter. Do not slip into saying 'This letter is a "sss"'. It isn't. It's an *s* (ess).

We are trying to make a clear distinction between the letter and its sound, just as there is a clear distinction between an animal and the sound or sounds it makes. If we are talking about a dog and want to emphasise this distinction, it makes a nonsense to call the animal a 'woof-woof' or a 'yap-yap' or a 'grrr', because it isn't. It is a dog and those are just examples of the sounds it can make. Incidentally, I find a dog a very useful animal when I am trying to explain that a letter may indicate different sounds or can be silent.

Trying to guess the sound from the letter name

Watch out for the child who relies on working out the sound of the letter from the letter name. This strategy works for most consonants but fails with *c*, *g*, *h*, *qu*, *w*, *y* and the vowels. His strategy will be shown up if we ask him for the sounds of letters and he tells us any of the following: that *u* is 'yuh' (from 'yoo'); *h* is 'chuh' (from 'aitch'); *w* is 'duh' (from 'double-yoo'); *y* is 'www' (from 'why'). Also suspect this strategy if he gives the soft sounds for *c* and *g* – in other words, if he says that the sound of *c* is 'sss' (which it can be when followed by *e*, *i* or *y*, but we want him to learn the 'kuh' sound first), and that the sound of *g* is 'juh' (which it is sometimes when followed by *e*, *i* or *y*, but we want him to learn the hard 'guh' sound first).

Why would he be relying on this strategy? He clearly has no difficulty in identifying initial sounds, considering that he has used that skill to work out his versions of letter sounds. Perhaps he has not made a strong enough link in his memory between a letter and its alphabet picture or pictures. See if you can get one of his family or another child in the class to help him memorise which goes with which. Once he knows that, he will be able to work out the letter sound correctly for himself.

> *Asked if she knew how to play I Spy, seven-year-old Chloe's face lit up.*
> *'Ooh, yes. I love playing that. I'll go first. I spy with my little eye something beginning with "sss".'*
> *She was very surprised when we failed to guess that she was thinking of 'window'.*

Difficulties with initial sounds

Does the child understand what we are asking him to do?

I Spy is a useful game to get the beginner reader to think of the initial sound of a word. Play it with letter sounds, not letter names. For example: I spy with my little eye something beginning with 'fff', or beginning with 'shhh'. Note that since the child is listening to the sound only, his guess of 'photo' is as valid as 'fish', and 'chef' as valid as 'shoe', always assuming there are such objects or pictures in sight.

However, what do we do when a child has difficulty with such a simple game? Chloe (above) was new to the school that day. When she made a 'sss' sound although she had chosen 'window', I reserved judgement about her hearing and intelligence, and made the task simpler: 'Chloe, here are two things, scissors and a ruler. I am going to say one of them. Listen carefully, and see if you can point to the one I choose before I finish saying it. Listen ... s-s-scissors.'

Chloe at first just guessed and pointed before I had even started. I explained again that it was a matter of listening. She eventually got the idea, and with practice learned to play I Spy normally. She was nearly eight years old and of average intelligence. When her school records caught up with her, it turned out that her progress had been badly affected by emotional factors, for which she had recently received psychiatric help.

Chapter 3

Problems over naming things

Mistakes can occur over names. If a child is not responding in a game of I Spy, is it because we are thinking of the mat, while the one in his home is always called a rug? Or have we chosen the thermometer and he has no idea what it is called? If this is likely to be a problem, what about having a session of naming all the objects in sight before starting the game?

This problem can also occur with picture alphabets and other pictures or objects that you use to teach phonics. Get into the habit of going through all of them with the children, making sure that everyone knows what to call them. Otherwise you may find a child busily learning that the letter *m* shows a 'duh' for 'Dad' rather than a 'mmm' for 'Man'.

Jason's error (see page 49) was my fault entirely. I had forgotten that he had been away when I had worked through the wall alphabet with the rest of the group, identifying the pictures. Not that I would have suspected then, in my early years as a teacher, that a child might have such a gap in his knowledge and/or vocabulary at eight years old.

Teaching early phonics using a collection of small objects

The simple game I describe here teaches children to distinguish initial sounds, but it is easy to adapt for other purposes, such as getting them to listen to final or middle sounds, or for teaching blending. You need a collection of small objects. Three-dimensional things are fun to use, and help motivation and understanding. They need to be familiar and easy to name, such as: a piece of string, a toothbrush, a battery, a button, a lipstick, a postage stamp, a key, a nail, a plastic spoon, a lid, zoo and farm animals, cars and other means of transport, various people such as a footballer and a Red Indian chief, and some things out of a doll's house.

Put out some of these objects and name each of them to make sure that everyone knows what each object is and what it is usually called. Now make the sound that starts the name of one or more of the objects. If the child can name an object

*Jason had a read-copy-and-draw card and was using it together with the wall alphabet which had been extended to include the sounds of **sh**, **ch** and **th**.*
He sounded puzzled. 'What's a fig, Miss?'
*I went over to see what card he was trying to read. It was 'a fish'. Remembering to praise what I could praise, I said, 'Well done, you have got the first two letters right. It does start with a "fi-" sound. It is just the end you need to think about again. Have another look at the **sh** [ess aitch] on the wall.'*
*I pointed to the **sh** card with a photograph of a very woolly sheep.*
When I came back again Jason was still making the word 'fig'.
*I pointed to the **sh** picture again. 'What's the name of that animal?'*
'It's a goat, ain't it, Miss?'
'No, it isn't a goat. Try again.'
'Well, it ain't a cow, and I'm bloody sure it ain't an 'orse. If it ain't a goat, I dunno what, Miss.'

beginning with that sound he wins the object for the duration of the game (on the understanding that he has to give it back when the game is over). 'I am thinking of something beginning with "chuh". What is it?' You may be thinking of the tiny chair or the chimpanzee for 'chuh', but be prepared for someone to pick the helicopter on the grounds that it can be called a chopper. He clearly understands the game.

Failing to guess the object

But what if the child picks the helicopter and says it is a helicopter, despite the fact that we have given him a 'chuh' sound? It may be enough just to clarify: 'No, helicopter starts with "hhh" – h-h-helicopter, but you have to find something that starts with "chuh". Chuh... chuh... which thing begins with "chuh"?' We can make it easier by reducing the number of objects to choose from.

Robin was so keen on winning the helicopter that he picked it hopefully each time, regardless of what initial sound I had given the group. When I realised what was happening, I changed the rules and said that from now on, if people guessed correctly three times running, they would be allowed to pick up not only those three objects, but a bonus one of their choice. Robin had first go, applied his mind and soon earned the helicopter as a bonus, thus establishing to my satisfaction that he was able to identify initial sounds correctly.

But what if a child cannot pick the right object, even with the bonus as an incentive? Make the task even simpler. Point to each object in turn and compare it with the given sound: 'Tell me when I come to the right one. Chuh... battery, chuh... horse, chuh... car, chuh... chair, chuh... zebra.'

What if he still does not succeed? Resort to two objects only, as I did with Chloe (see page 47).

The child who is not learning

Some children choose not to concentrate on listening to the sounds and comparing them, but, instead, watch out for the slightest indication from us that we have reached the right object. If we unconsciously pause slightly or change our words or tone or the direction of our look, these children will get the answer right but will have failed to learn what we are trying to teach them. We have to outdo them in cunning. Work up a rhythm, almost chanting, and carry on past the correct object if the children do not spot it. Then repeat it all again: 'Come on, one of these has got to be the right one. Which one is it? Which one starts with the same sound?' Thrown back on comparing the sounds, a child usually does not need to hear them a third time before getting it right.

Memorising letter sounds

Learning from phonic alphabets

Does a child have difficulty in remembering the sounds of the alphabet? Here are some suggestions which may help.

- Have a phonic alphabet strip in clear view on the classroom wall. Go through this frequently with the children: name of letter, sound of letter, name of what is pictured. Our aim is for the children to over-learn so that they will not forget. Keep an eye on the child you are particularly trying to teach. Is he actively trying to learn? Just watching you and listening is not enough. Expect him to say or mouth the letter name, letter sound and name of the object after you, in order to help him remember. And make sure he lives up to your expectations.

- Build up a strong visual link in memory between the picture and the letter by frequently getting the children to recall them together. Tell the children to turn away from the wall alphabet. Then show them a letter on card or somewhere in the room, and ask them to tell you its associated picture (*a*, apple; *b*, balloon, or whatever). Another time, do this the other way round by showing them the picture without the letter (if you can), or by asking 'What letter goes with the picture of the ...?'

- Link each letter with other objects and words as well, so that, for example, a child usually thinks of *r* with the picture of the rabbit but also associates the letter with rulers, rubbish, his friend Richard and 'Round the rugged rocks the ragged rascals ran'. A child who links a letter with only one picture may get muddled. He may forget what the picture is, and so connect *r* with 'hhh' for 'hare' instead of 'rrr' for rabbit. He may even not realise that we are talking about *sound*, and so he learns that *r* has something to do with a rabbit, but does not know what.

Remembering by writing and saying

Encourage a child to say or mouth the sounds of the letters as he writes them. He will then be combining hearing and the movement of his lips and tongue with the rest of his learning. Using input from several senses at a time will improve his ability to memorise. But our main object is to get the child to associate sight with sound, the lines and squiggles on the paper with the sounds of English.

Suggestions for revising letter sounds

Sets of cards with single letters, with or without matching sets of pictures, can be useful for teaching and revising letter sounds. Cards can be obtained from educational suppliers. Here are a few ideas for using them to teach a small group.

- Collect together some small familiar objects and place them on a table. Now choose letter cards that match their initial sounds. For example, if you put out the following six things – a lipstick, a zip fastener, a button, a stamp, a penny and a pencil (the last two starting with the same sound), you need five cards only, showing *l*, *z*, *b*, *s* and *p*. Show a letter silently. Ask the children to find an object that has a name starting with the same sound as the letter. Tell them that there may be more than one object that matches. (This is an adaptation of a game for teaching initial sounds, described in detail on pages 48-50.)

- Play a variation of I Spy. Show a letter silently. Can the children think of something in the room starting with that sound?

- Choose a small number of letters and matching pictures. Also choose two pictures that do not match any of the letters. Mix them all up, put them face up on a table and ask the children to pair them up by sound. Warn them not to get caught out by the extra pictures.

- If you have a set of cards with letters on one side and their matching pictures on the reverse, choose letters that you particularly want to revise and put them out on the table, letter side up (neatly or scattered). Each child in turn chooses a letter, says what its sound is, and then turns the card over to reveal the picture on the back. We are aiming to make children as independent as possible, so encourage the child whose turn it is and the rest of the group to work out for themselves from the picture whether the sound was right. Letters the children get right they win. Letters that they find difficult are put to one side to be shown later again and again until the children know and win them.

M says 'mmm'. N says 'nnn'.
One little boy thought he was deaf because he could not hear the letters saying anything.

Does he think he is deaf?

Letters do not talk, but teachers say they do. '*M* says "mmm". *R* says "rrr"'. A child may take this literally and conclude that he is deaf because he cannot hear the letters saying anything. Extremely unlikely? No, apparently not. When I first heard of a child who thought he was deaf like this, I told my next group of seven- and eight-year-olds about him. One boy nodded sympathetically and said that until very recently he, too, had thought himself deaf for the same reason.

We can change our own words to avoid muddling a child in this way, but we cannot ensure that he will not hear the puzzling statement from others. So we need to explain that the letters are not actually speaking, and that when people say '*M* says "mmm"', they don't mean that the *m* is sitting there on the paper making a 'mmm' noise. They mean that *m* is the way of writing down a 'mmm' sound in a spoken word.

Winnie, sounding out triumphantly: 'Kuh-a-tuh ... DOG!!!'

Difficulties with sounding out and blending

Not understanding the task

Once a child knows his letter sounds we want him to learn to 'sound out' and 'blend'. That means looking at the letters in turn, saying their sounds, and running the sounds together in order to guess the word. Note the word 'guess'. Teachers ask: 'What does "kuh-a-tuh" make?' Well, it does not make 'dog', but it does not make 'cat' either. It does not *make* anything. We are expecting the child to make a mental leap from the approximate letter sounds to the whole word.

When Winnie (above) sounded out the word 'cat' and decided the word was 'dog', she clearly did not understand what she was being asked to do with the letter sounds, but she was doing her best. She probably remembered seeing 'cat' in a group of words with pictures and, without phonics to help her, had matched it with the wrong picture in that group.

When a child makes an attempt like Winnie's, we can respond to what she or he is doing right. 'That's right, kuh-a-tuh, and you are right, it *is* an animal, a pet, but it's not "dog". "Dog" would be duh-o-guh, but this is KUH-a-tuh' (and here we emphasise the first sound, the sound of *c*, and let the other two trail away). 'Listen very carefully, KUH-a-tuh. Can you think of a pet that sounds like that? KUH-a-tuh.' (Or we combine the *c* with the vowel if that is the school's usual practice, and say CA-tuh).

But there is an easier way to teach a child blending.

Learning blending without having to read

We can make the task of blending easier if we sound out the word for the children while they just listen, maybe with their

54

eyes shut, and then try to guess it. No words to look at, no letter sounds to remember – just listening and blending. (However, if children are finding the task difficult, suggest that they repeat the sounds to themselves, several times if necessary, mouthing them quietly.)

Emphasise the initial sound. (If a child keeps getting the word the wrong way round, see page 56, 'Reversing what he has sounded out'.)

At least to begin with, give the children some clue as to the type of word we are going to sound out. 'What animal am I thinking about? A *M-ou-se* [MMM-ou-sss]'.

The Action Game (see page 22) can be adapted for this purpose. Instead of showing the words, just sound them out and get the children to do the action. Demonstrate first: 'I am going to touch a bit of myself. Listen carefully, and see if you can guess which bit.' Begin slowly to move your hand in the right direction while saying: 'I am going to touch my *N-o-se* [NNN-oh-zzz]... Did you guess it? Let's try another one. I am going to touch my *N-e-ck* [NNN-e-k]'. etc.

Once the children have got the idea, make them do the action. 'Touch your *H-ea-d*' or 'Show me your *L-e-g*.' (Or: *N-o-se*; *L-i-p*; *KN-ee*; *N-e-ck*; *CH-ee-k*; *CH-i-n*; *F-a-ce*; *F-oo-t*; *T-ee-th*; *T-oe-s*; *M-ou-th*; *H-ee-l*; *WR-i-st*; *TH-u-mb*, etc.)

Watch for the child who is not bothering to blend because he has worked out an easier method of getting the answer.

● Is he just copying the others? Move him to the front and give him a turn on his own.

● Is he a dab hand at picking up the slightest clue from us, such as the direction of our gaze? When thinking about what to blend next, avoid looking in that direction. Deliberately look at other things before speaking again.

● Is he just listening to the initial sound and then guessing without trying to blend at all? Outmanoeuvre him by including in the game two or more words starting with the same sound (*nose, knee, neck,* or *head, hair, hand, heel* or *chin, cheek, chest*). Sometimes deliberately look at the wrong one – look at knees while saying *N-o-se*.

These children's street-wise ploys are a fundamental cause of their failure to learn what we have all been trying to teach them. It is essential that we circumvent such unhelpful tactics.

Here are some more ideas for a blending version of the Action Game: 'I want you to do something. *H-o-p. S-i-t. J-u-m-p. C-l-a-p* (or *CL-a-p* or *CLA-p*). Pretend to use a *C-o-mb.* Pretend to *D-i-g'*, etc.

Once the children are confident at this, move on to sounding out words without giving any clue first. This is harder for them and we want them still to succeed, so stick to the names of familiar things that you are sure they know.

Finally, remember that if the children are to succeed in sounding out words for themselves, they obviously need to know the sounds of the letters well in the first place. Provided they do, then all this blending practice should begin to pay off.

Incorrectly adding extra syllables

When sounding out, does the child work out *b-i-g* as 'bigger', or make *s-t-a-m-p* into something like 'Sir Tammerper'? He is probably saying the letter sounds with an emphatic 'uh' or 'er'. Point out that this is causing the difficulty, and encourage him to pronounce them more helpfully. (See Appendix, page 156, 'Saying the sounds of consonants'.) Encourage him also to make the most of clues from context and syntax so that he does not have to rely on phonics alone to work out a word.

Reversing what he has sounded out

Does he sound out a word correctly but say a word starting with the end letter? For example, does he sound out *c-a-t* and say 'tack', or *d-o-g* and say 'god'? He is remembering the last sound, the sound 'nearest' to him. He will probably get over this if he always emphasises the first one or two letters as he sounds it out: *C-a-t,* or *CA-t.* Remind him also to use all the clues to the word that he can get from context and syntax. An isolated word will be more difficult.

A child who often has difficulty getting a word the right way round in ordinary speech may need to be referred to a speech therapist if that has not happened already. If, however, the difficulty has only cropped up over sounding out, and emphasising the first sound has not overcome it, there is something else you might try – but only if it interests you and you have a spare moment. Try getting the child to link time with space and gross movement by 'walking' the sounding-out with him. Write the letters of the word wide apart along the length of the board, or place separate letters in line on the floor. Walk with the child past each letter, getting him to sound out each one with you and say the whole word at the finish. If he is interested and co-operative, repeat this several times and see if it helps him. But I urge you to drop the idea if you catch yourself doing it in a spirit of 'I'm going to succeed with this child even if it kills me.' Stress is no solution to speech problems.

The child who avoids sounding out

It seems that the very last thing some children will do is to sound out a word, and then only under duress. The child's weakness is compounded if, when reading to himself, he is not over-bothered when the word he guesses does not make sense in context, e.g. when he misreads 'bad' for 'bell', or 'birthday' for 'button'.

How can we improve his word attack? A more interesting reading book would be a start. Here are some other ideas.

● Try bigger print. It makes it easier to analyse words.

● Check that he knows his letter sounds and pronounces them well. (See pages 51-53 and 155-158.)

● Can he blend easily? If not, see page 54.

- Encourage him to mouth words as he copies them, stretching each word out as he says it so that it starts and finishes at the same time as his writing.

- Give a beginner reader simple but funny 'read-copy-and-draw' cards to read and carry out on his own. Think up rather bizarre pictures for him to draw so that he cannot rely solely on guessing words from context. Examples: a pig on a red rug; a fox in a net; six hats on a bed; a vet and ten rats; a red bib on a duck; a flag on a pram; a crab on a box; a sock on a dog; a man lost in a fog.

- See if you can find the kind of work sheet that has a picture and several words to choose from, for example: a picture of a cat, and the words 'cut', 'cup', 'cat', 'can'.

- Show a more advanced reader that sounding out is not so difficult as he thinks. Use hyphens to divide interesting long words into syllables, and ask him to read them. Also cut up words into syllables which he then has to put in the right order.

- Above all, make sure the child gets lots of success and praise. Praise any attempt he makes to work out a word. (See page 14 on helpful ways of praising.)

Syllables

Children need to be able to break words up into syllables, not only for reading but also for spelling (see pages 72, 115-116, 136 and 143-144). If a child has difficulty understanding syllables, ask him to clap the 'lumps of sound' in a word and tell you how many times he has clapped. Start him with easy words, such as 'chimp-an-zee', 'pho-to-graph' or 'foot-ball', all of which have a clear last syllable. Some children find it hard at first to identify a one-syllable word, and try to justify extra claps by sounding it out.

Poems, comic verse and nursery rhymes with very obvious regular metre and rhyme are useful. Emphasising the metre breaks up words into their syllables. Encourage the children not just to listen to poetry but to learn to recite it, articulating each syllable distinctly as it plays its part in rhythm and rhyme.

Weaving phonics into other word-attack skills

We need constantly to keep in mind that phonics is best used in combination with other word-attack skills. Many of the activities discussed in this chapter have to do with teaching phonic skills in isolation, but we need to show the child how to use phonics in ordinary reading – not instead of the other word-attack skills he has been using but in addition to them.

When a child comes across a new word in his reading, he cannot tell in advance if his limited phonics (or, indeed, any amount of phonics) will be able to help him work it out. So, when we hear him read and we notice that it is no use his trying phonics on the next word, do we tell him so? It is certainly tempting to rush in 'helpfully' to 'save' him from potential failure, tempting to tell him straightaway what the word is, or to advise him not to bother with phonics this time but just rely on context. But is this really the type of help he needs just now? When he is reading on his own, the only way he is going to find out if phonics will help him with a word is to try it. Therefore what he needs to know is *what to do next when he cannot read a word.*

Suggest that he goes on reading. The next few words or sentences may make it clear what the word was. The word may not be worth agonizing over at this moment, anyway, provided he understands the rest of what he is reading, and he may be able to read it when he meets it next time in more helpful context. However, sometimes a word is so crucial to his understanding of the passage that he begins to lose comprehension. What if he cannot ask anyone at this point what the word is? He can comfort and reassure himself by remembering what we have said in the past – that we too have often got stuck on difficult words, words that sometimes we have never even heard of. (See 'ceilidh', page 37.)

Chapter Four

Context, grammar and punctuation

In this chapter we consider the important part that context and grammar can play in helping to identify a word when reading.

The child who reads 'The dog wagged his ...' and then laboriously sounds out 't-a-i-l' or 't-ai-l' is clearly not using the words he has already read to help him guess the fifth one. He has not used context.

Similarly, the child who reads 'Higher and higher ...' and misreads the next word as 'them' is not using grammar to filter out a guess which could not possibly be right. His guess may be very close visually (for example if the actual word is 'the', 'then', or 'their'), but grammatically he should never have considered it. If he has a reasonably good command of English as his mother tongue, his intuitive knowledge of English syntax (the rules for the grammatical arrangement of words) should have rejected such a word from the start. However, if he has never heard such a construction, never heard 'Higher and higher the kite flew' or a similar example, he has lost comprehension and cannot therefore use context to make an intelligent guess at the next word.

Also in this chapter we consider punctuation, and the use of italic or bold type to indicate emphasis. A child has a great gap in comprehension if he does not realise the differences between 'He is wrong', 'He is wrong?', 'He is wrong!' and '*He* is wrong.'

Confusing visually similar words

When reading, does the child substitute a word for another that looks very much the same? If he misreads 'house' as 'home', it sounds as if he could be reading for meaning, although slightly carelessly, but if he confuses 'house' and 'horse', that is a different matter. For example, suppose he reads 'Emma loved riding and spent all her spare time looking after her aunt's house' (instead of 'horse'), he has not used context to help.

Guessing is OK

We aim to teach the child that reading can become much easier and quicker if he uses contextual and grammatical cues, and we show him how to combine these with phonics to home in on a word. A child may have been reprimanded at home or at school for guessing. We now not only encourage him to guess, but assure him that all good readers use guessing or prediction as a valuable part of their reading skills. We can show him what we mean if we remove the worry of reading and get him just to listen and guess as he takes part in the Context Game.

The Context Game

Outline of the game

Begin to read a story to a group but stop every now and again to ask the children to guess what the next word is going to be. Then reveal the initial sound of the word, and let them revise their guesses before telling them the word itself. Our aim is to show them that their guesses are sensible and sometimes correct, and even more likely to be correct if they use a little phonics to help.

A story that they have not heard is best. It needs to be well within the interest and language level of the group. At the same time it will probably have to be well above their reading level, as we need good ordinary English and an interesting story of the type not met within the limits of early reading books. Traditional tales usually have a predictable pattern of language and plot, and are therefore a better choice than off-beat stories.

If the story happens to start with 'Once upon a ...', then the weakest reader can start the ball rolling, and get instant success. Little else at the beginning of a story is going to be easy to predict. 'Once upon a time there was a ...?' has very wide possibilities: princess, country, dragon, boy, old, beautiful, wicked, very, etc. The story becomes more predictable as it develops.

Accept every sensible suggestion with equal approval. 'Yes, it could be that.' There are no winners and losers. It is not a competition. We are trying to show them that guessing is worthwhile, and that their guesses are on the right lines. After all, if we read 'Once, long ago, in a cave deep in the mountains there lived a ...', no one is likely to suggest 'television set'.

A stupid guess?

What about a guess that appears to be stupid? Follow it up. Ask the child to explain what he had in mind. Perhaps he misheard what we read, or needs help with grammar, or is mispronouncing something. Or is he the intelligent boy in the class who is always playing the fool, and on this occasion has suggested an obscure word that could be just remotely possible? Point out to him: 'That's possible, but highly unlikely. The whole point of this is to pick the most probable.' Then stretch him with a more difficult challenge, such as: 'He had spread out all his treasures on an open space, not ...' (thinking? without? far? in?). Ask him to justify his guess in terms of how the story has developed so far.

Only the grammatically possible

Keep the children strictly to the text while still accepting possibilities of how the story is going to develop. Suppose someone suggests 'elephant' to follow 'The next animal he met was a ...'. We need to take this up and explain: 'Yes, it might be an elephant, but that cannot be the next word. We say "*an* elephant" and what we've got is: "The next animal he met was *a*" something. If you guess he met an elephant, then maybe it is "*a big* elephant" or "*a friendly* elephant". That would make sense.'

Refining the guess

After they have guessed, start revealing what the actual word was, using the initial letter or letters, and ask them to refine their guesses. 'You have suggested it could be a rabbit or a horse or a tiger. I'll tell you what the word in the book starts with. The letter *d* [dee]. So it is an animal starting with a 'duh' sound. What do you think it is? ... Dog? Let's see. [Sound out:] *d-o-n-k* ... Yes, it's donkey, Adrian. Well done.'

Pick up the thread of the story by going back slightly in the text when starting to read again.

Keep the game short. Stop before getting far into the story. Who wants interruptions when the story is getting exciting? Either treat the game as a 'preview' and promise to read the whole story from beginning to end at story-time, or finish reading it normally to them here and now, but only as an 'extra' story. Their daily story-time is sacrosanct. Reading games have no place in it.

Predictability

Predictability makes for easy reading. Factors like a jokey or bizarre story or an unfamiliar grammatical construction or frequent pronouns (e.g. he, they, she, him, we, hers) can make guessing harder. Speed of reading is likely to fall, and errors increase. Even an experienced adult reader is more likely to predict the next word incorrectly. He can be on the point of saying the obvious one he expects, before he realises that the actual word is something else. He corrects himself, often with only a slight hesitation to betray him. Using writing of this kind is not helpful when we are trying to teach children that they can guess usefully. A high degree of predictability is best for the game.

Reading on

Once the children are confident about guessing the next word from what they have already heard, we can introduce them to the idea of guessing the word from what follows.

We read out: '"The doctor took out his ..."' and then we explain: 'The next word is a long one. Let's see if it helps to go on reading, and then try to guess. I'll start again. "The doctor took out his ... and listened to Grandpa's chest. He told him to take a deep breath."

'Has anyone any idea what the word is? Yes, Daniel, you are right. It is going to be that thing, that instrument that doctors put in their ears so that they can listen to our chests, but does anyone know what it is called? ... It begins with "st" [stuh]. Yes, stethoscope. Well done.'

I do not do much of this in the Context Game because it slows the story down, and anyway it is easier when the child can see the words. When we hear him read in future, and he gets stuck on a word, we just need to remind him that reading on a little may give him the help he needs. We should remind him to try reading on *even when we can see it will not help this time*. We are trying to instil good strategies. We are not promising that they will always be successful.

Cloze procedure

We can use a form of Cloze procedure to give children more practice in using surrounding words to help narrow the possibilities for an unknown word. Words are deleted from a piece of writing, and the children discuss what words are omitted, or they can complete individual work sheets and then have a general discussion. When Cloze procedure was first taken up by schools deletions were made at strict intervals (for example, every tenth word), but our purpose now is best served by deleting judiciously, according to what level of challenge we wish to give the child or the group.

Not enough language and general knowledge?

Even a native English speaker will find it difficult to use contextual and grammatical cues if his language development is poor and he lacks general knowledge. Such a child needs particular help with reading. (See pages 89-91, 'When language development and general knowledge need to be greater', and page 90, 'Peer-tutoring'.)

Punctuation

Not noticing punctuation

Early reading books may contain very little punctuation, and anyway the child has to concentrate so hard on reading the words that he is likely to ignore smaller marks on the paper. Now he needs to become aware of them and of what they are called, and to learn what they are used for.

Here is a suggestion for practising the identification of punctuation marks with a small group. Make copies for everyone of a well-punctuated passage from a book, or write the passage on the board. Divide the group into two teams, A and B. Each child plays in turn, a child from team A, then one from team B, then another from A, etc. The aim of the game is to name the next punctuation mark in the text and thus gain a point for one's team (one punctuation mark a turn). If the child omits a mark, or calls it something else, or takes too long remembering, either tell them what it is or let the turn pass to the other team. Alternatively, the children can play against us and we get a point if they are wrong or take too long, but we play it this way only if they are certain to win. We want each child to finish up motivated, successful and more aware of punctuation.

If you use copies of a printed text for this activity, it is useful to pick a passage that contains an example of italics used for emphasis, which you can then point out. (Other uses for italics can be taught later.) Unless attention is drawn to italics, some children fail to notice the difference in type or else do not learn the significance.

Not knowing when to use punctuation

Here is a suggested activity for teaching a small group when to use punctuation marks.

Find a passage that has the punctuation marks you want to teach, or write one specially for the purpose. You are going to read this to the children and ask them to decide what punctuation marks are needed.

Provide each child with a set of the punctuation marks,

every mark and its name written large on a separate sheet of paper (for example: ? Question mark). Also, if you wish, provide each child with a sheet marked 'Capital letter' (to follow full stops).

Begin to read. When you come to a punctuation mark, tell the children that one is needed there, but then read on a little so that they know what follows. Now go back, reread up to the punctuation mark in question, and ask the children to hold up whichever mark they think is the right one. In this way we can see who is understanding, and who is still in a fog. For example, you read: '"... until she came to a big box" – we need a punctuation mark here, but wait to hear what comes next. "... She tried to pick it up ..." So, show me what we need after "a big box". Yes, a full stop. Then what do we need? ... Mmm? After a full stop? Yes, of course, a capital letter.' How much text you need to repeat each time will vary.

As you read, give as much help as you can. For example, drop your voice for a full stop, over-act an exclamation, and change your voice for reported speech (by whispering or adopting an accent, perhaps).

You can change this game to practise the use just of capital letters, or just of the apostrophe, particularly if some children at present add an apostrophe to every word ending in s. Each child needs a card on which is written 'Capital letter' or 'Apostrophe' as appropriate. Find or think up a suitable passage to read. Read each sentence or phrase slowly twice. On the second reading the children hold up their cards if and when they think the card applies. Invent some system for scoring if you wish. For example, tell them that there are ten stepping stones to get from one side of a river to the other. Draw the river and the stones on the board. Tell the children that there are similarly ten capital letters (or apostrophes) in the story. Each one they spot correctly means that they can advance onto the next stepping stone. Show their progress. Can they get right across the river?

Chapter Five

Sight words

This chapter looks at the difficulties some children have in memorising words, and suggests ways of helping. All beginner readers need right from the start to build up a stock of words that they recognise by sight, especially words that occur very frequently in early reading. As explained in Chapter 3 (page 35), they need this sight recognition vocabulary even if they are learning to use phonics, and the sooner they acquire it the better.

Not necessarily learnt by sight

Wider ways of learning

A child may fail to recognise words that he has seen many, many times before. If there is any suspicion in our minds that the child might have an undiagnosed eyesight problem, we can suggest that the child be tested by an optometrist. But that apart, bear in mind that although a word has to be recognised by sight, it does not necessarily have to be taught by sight alone, in the way some parents try to teach their baby by showing words on flash cards. We can offer more extensive ways of learning.

- Present each word in context, so the child learns it as part of a phrase or a sentence. (For example: 'My mum <u>can't</u> swim.')

- Make sure that the child knows the names of all the letters in the word so that he can learn it by spelling it out letter by letter if that is his choice.

- Teach him to notice the shape of the word: its length, and whether it is flat or has letters sticking up or down in certain places. See if there is a computer game available which will teach him to match words with their word shapes.

- Get the child to trace a large written version of the word, using a finger or a pencil, and then to practise writing the word with a finger in sand or on his knee or on the palm of his other hand. Get him to say the word each time. This not only links the sound of the word with the action and look of writing it, but ensures that the child is not practising just a series of meaningless movements.

- Explain how to analyse the word using phonics, to help memorise it even if it is irregular (for example, learning 'who' by pronouncing it 'www-ho' to rhyme with 'go').

- See to it that the child copies the word more than once, not on its own but contained in a short phrase or sentence so that he learns it in context. He needs to copy in good handwriting (to keep the shape of words), while saying each word in a prolonged fashion to synchronise with the writing of it.

- Select some words the child needs to learn. Write them on separate pieces of card in very large letters. Place them on the floor so that the child can step over or jump over each word while saying it aloud. Memorising through big, energetic movements can be particularly helpful to some children. It is like hammering in the memory – in the same way that some people thump one fist into the palm of their other hand or into their thigh or knee when they are trying to remember something very important. 'I must [thump] remember [thump] to pick up those keys [thump] first thing tomorrow [thump].'

- Use repeated recall. Select some words you want a small group to learn. Think up ways of getting the children to recall these words repeatedly. For example, write the words in a circle on the board and then 'go round the clock' (or 'the world') chanting each word with the children several times before each child has a go on his own. Or write each word on a separate piece of card and place all the cards face down. Children then take turns to choose a card, turn it over and say the word. If correct, they win it. If not, you say what it is, and keep the card to be practised again later on. Another suggestion is to provide a duplicate set of the words on cards and play word snap. Any activity that increases the number of times a child recalls a word will strengthen his memory of it.

- Make it more rewarding for the child to remember than not to remember. Give him attention and approval when he succeeds or when he is clearly concentrating and trying to learn, but give him little if any when he is clearly not trying and/or when he is very trying. Listen to your gut instinct if it tells you that a child is making a spurious attempt to remember (for example, screwing up his eyes and biting his lip in an exaggerated way as if play-acting). Try not to reward such behaviour by showing interest or irritation but keep on the look-out for any desirable learning behaviour of his that you can reinforce positively.

Learning by copying

It is worth remembering that some little girls love to sit at home and assiduously copy pages and pages from books, even though they may not understand what they are copying. A boy who is very weak on sight words might do worse than follow their example. If he is motivated enough to try this, he will at least be looking at words more closely, repeatedly copying common strings of letters, and something might 'rub off'. Also, the extra practice might speed up his handwriting and help his spelling. (See page 125, 'Good handwriting helps with spelling'.)

Chapter 5

Getting letters and words the wrong way round

Does the child still frequently get letters and words the wrong way round? Does he mix up *d* with *p* and/or *b*, *m* with *w*, *saw* with *was*, *felt* with *left*, and so on? We attack this on a broad front, with energy.

Reassurance

Parents need to know that sometimes getting muddled about the way round or up a letter goes is part of the normal process of learning to read. A banana is a banana, no matter which way up or round it is, but two-dimensional letters are different: it does matter how they are orientated. Parents may be justifiably worried, however, if their child is still having considerable problems with orientation after two or more years of schooling. They may become convinced that their child is dyslexic. Bland reassurance is extremely unhelpful and so is the build-up of an emotionally charged situation. The parents are entitled to expect us to be working on their child's problem energetically and with competence. Unless the child has been properly assessed by an educational psychologist and diagnosed as dyslexic, let us keep an open mind about his orientation difficulties. Let us instead concentrate on doing, and being seen to be doing, a good professional job in trying to help him get over those difficulties.

Keeping the door open

Let us help the parents and the child to keep an open mind too. When we are told 'He always mixes up "was" and "saw"', we can quietly introduce a slight but significant change later in the conversation, like this: 'You pointed out that he has had a problem over reversing words.' In the same way, when the child says he is no good at reading and/or spelling, we nod understandingly and acknowledge that he has not found that easy up to now. In both cases we have not accepted a diagnosis of a permanent condition but have made an amended, limited statement that the child has had great difficulties in the past. We have opened up the possibility that from now on things may change. We now look at what we can do to facilitate this.

Letter formation and joined-up handwriting

Does he form his letters correctly? If not, see pages 98-102 of Chapter 7, Handwriting. You will find detailed suggestions there on multi-sensory learning and on what to try if that is not effective. In accordance with those suggestions, you might start on the child's difficulties as follows.

Writing with his finger   Have the child practise writing letters with his finger in sand or on the carpet, and also on his knee or the palm of his other hand. If he finds it very difficult to get a particular letter right, ask the parents to help if they will.

Writing on the child's back   Suggest that when a child finds a letter very difficult, his parents try writing it with a finger on his back before he himself writes it or makes it in the air. This may help him to visualise the letter without a mistake in orientation.

Tracing letters with a finger   Provide the parents with a model of the letter the child finds difficult, making the letter large enough to be traced accurately with a finger. Mark the letter with different coloured dots to show where the child should start and finish, and with arrows showing the path he should take. Ask the parents to get him to practise tracing this model letter with his finger, and also with a pencil using tracing paper or cheap greaseproof paper.

Learning to join letters   Joined-up writing can help some children considerably in overcoming their orientation confusions. So if a child is not already using joined-up handwriting, try introducing him to it, but not until he is clear where each letter on its own starts and stops. If he does not know letter boundaries, he can get awfully confused by the joining strokes.

Practising words in joined-up writing   Provide him with models of words he finds difficult. Write them in joined-up writing large enough to be traced over properly with a finger. Mark them in the same way as suggested for individual letters. Get the child to trace over the writing with his finger and then with a pencil using tracing paper. Show him how to talk himself through the task so that he learns by a combination of sight, hearing, touch and muscle movements of mouth and hand, and understands what he is doing. Seek help from the parents along the same lines as for letter formation.

Using context and phonics

When reading, a child who has difficulty with orientation needs to use all the help he can get from context and grammar and a good phonic attack. (See pages 36, 44 and 60.)

When writing freely or just copying, does he say the word as he writes, prolonging the sound to synchronise with each syllable and group of letters? He needs to, to curb his tendency to think one word while unthinkingly writing another. When copying, he needs to learn to check his own work as he goes along, with a finger on the original and another finger or his pencil on his copy. (See page 120, 'Self-checking what he has copied'.)

Left-to-right movement

When reading, can he sweep confidently from left to right, moving his finger along the words as he reads them? If not, then is there some further help we can give him to establish the right direction? In the absence of a useful scar, mole, or other distinguishing mark on one of his hands, what can we suggest the child uses? Depending on which hand he writes with, can he remember left-to-right in terms of 'pull' or 'push'? Or, using his classroom or his bedroom, can he visualise left-to-right as walking from the window to the door, or whatever is appropriate? What about his having a ruler with pictures stuck at each end: on the left a person walking towards his house on the right? Or a man on a motor bike heading for a chequered flag? Or a boy heading for an ice-cream? It may be worthwhile consulting colleagues in the infant school who will have games and puzzles to help establish orientation. Even if these do not prove suitable for an older child, they may spark off ideas of our own.

Getting down to it

Finally, does a child with orientation difficulties give himself enough time to think? Do we allow him enough time to think? If he knows he has a problem distinguishing 'was' from 'saw', he needs to stop when he meets one of them and *apply his mind.* Have we told him that we expect him to do so? Does he understand what to do? Time is not of the essence here, but marshalling all his word-attack skills certainly is.

When reading, has he checked that he is moving his finger from left to right? Has he checked that the initial sound of the word on the page matches the initial sound of the word that he thinks it is? Has he checked against a picture alphabet? Above all, has he checked that the word makes sense in context?

Reinforcing success

The child has had a marked problem over orientation up to now, and perhaps has been getting a lot of attention over it, particularly if the parents have become very worried. It may help him if we apparently almost ignore his mistakes, and concentrate on his successes not only in literacy but in other areas of school life. Note the word 'apparently'. Of course we take his orientation difficulties very seriously and tackle them with all the expertise and empathy we can, but this includes trying to defuse the situation. We need to help the child to relax, feel valued as a person, and enjoy attention and appreciation as a normal member of the class.

Chapter 5

The child who is failing to learn

Let us consider, as we do several times elsewhere in this book, the child who is in danger of escaping our rescue net, the child who customarily slips through each lesson effortlessly, unmarked by learning.

Learning and over-learning

This child has yet again failed to remember a word that we have every reason to expect him to know by now. It is not sufficient just to tell him it and carry on. We have barely stirred his mind if we have merely insisted that he repeat the correct word. He repeats it with minimum effort, and thereafter switches off as usual, unless we return again and again to the word, pouncing on him unexpectedly, demanding that he identify it each time. He may well protest indignantly that we have asked him already and that he has had his turn. It is not fair, and we are just picking on him, and so on. How we react is crucial.

All this time in school and so little gained by it? He deserves our compassion – and our sense of humour. We are not much good as teachers if an ordinary school child of seven, eight or more thinks the only reason we have asked him to repeat something is that we are showing animosity. It is high time we got across the idea that of course we have picked on him – to give him an extra chance to memorise, and that we do the same for anyone else who keeps forgetting some particular thing. And we apologise for not having explained before that repeating things over and over again like this even when you know the answer is a special technique called over-learning, which helps people to remember for a very long time, perhaps all their lives ... And what was that word again? Excellent.

And we do not leave it there, either. We ask him again at the end of the lesson, and when he is leaving for home, and we do our best to remember to ask him the next day, too. Repeated recall and attempted recall like this over intervals of hours, days, weeks, strengthens the memory – and our warm approval sweetens it.

The child who plays the fool

But what if he decided to play the fool when we asked him the word the first time and he did not know it? If he habitually plays for laughs in order to escape, he may be resistant to changing his attitude. He feels embarrassed and scared, and does not want to lose face. He may work better as a member of a team, so we can try dividing the group into teams competing with one another. His team will expect him to pull his weight, and this may get him going.

Contrariwise, he may work better on his own, so we can try him on a suitable interactive computer game for learning basic sight words, if one is available. He may respond well to interacting just with the computer, especially if the game is designed to give him a very satisfactory response to a correct answer. Make sure that he can play it alone in safety, with no risk of someone sneaking up and jeering, 'You're a moron! Don't you even know that word?!'

Children hungry for success

One group of children I knew were at first resistant to repeated questions, but eventually developed a game of their own that they begged to play each time. Standing in a line at the door at the end of the lesson, they wanted to be asked simple questions in turn. If they answered correctly they could leave, and if incorrectly they had to go to the end of the line to try again. They expected to be asked things that they had only just mastered or nearly mastered that lesson, interspersed with more general questions.

How do you spell *who*?
What day of the week is it?
What are two threes?
What does *y-o-u* spell?
What letter comes next after A, B, C, D, E?
What is the top word on the list over there?
How do we write the letter *d*? Show me in the air.

Chapter 5

And for the brighter children in the group:

> If today was Saturday, what was the day before yesterday?
> What word is spelt *e-y-e*?
> What comes before *v* in the alphabet?
> Multiply 6 by 2, and then take away 3. What are you left with?
> Think of the word *two*, as in 'two things'. How do we write it with joined-up writing? Show me with your finger in the air.

They loved these questions that they could nearly always get right, and over the weeks many useful things were practised, and gaps revealed and filled. The children soon discovered, however, that there was one snag in the game – that if they got the answer right they had to leave. They often ignored this rule and went back to the end of the line anyway so that they could enjoy success a second time.

Children can be desperately hungry for success. They need a chance to feast themselves on it. How often do we manage to pitch work for a low-achieving child at a level where he can achieve success at least 80-90 per cent of the time? And how do we gauge success?

Chapter Six

Reading:
the general picture

Pulling the whole thing together

In earlier chapters we have looked at ways of improving a child's understanding of what reading is all about, and at ways of helping him to develop particular word-attack skills. His ability to read is also affected by his handwriting, copying and spelling skills, and we shall come to these later. Now we look at some other aspects of reading. These do not include readability levels, reading tests and reading ages, nor a list of recommended books. You can find that information elsewhere.

Although there has been a massive amount of research, no one really knows how people learn to read. Many children teach themselves, and, without any training, many mothers, even barely literate ones, do a good job of teaching their children to read at home. Yet all too many people leave school without adequate reading skills, after many years in our professional hands. Considering the differing research findings, theories and swings of fashion in teaching methods over the years, I sometimes think that we are lucky that some children learn to read despite our well-meaning efforts to teach them! I reckon we can do with a spot of humility and a strong sense of humour.

Getting reading off the ground

Can he match words to print?

If a child has been at school for some two years or more and yet is still virtually a non-reader, can he at least match the words on the page with the words he hears? For example, if we read 'There were three pirates', can he point to each word in turn on the page? When we read 'Each pirate had a knife', can he point out which word must be 'pirate' or 'had'? Or is he having difficulty in distinguishing between words, acting as if each syllable is a new word, or as if he hears two or more words as one? If so, we can accept his difficulty and support him by saying, 'Working out where one word ends and the other begins is not easy. I will try to make it clearer.' Then make a clearer distinction between each word as you say it, 'pointing' the words more obviously with your voice. Leave a sufficient gap after each short phrase to give him plenty of time to work out the corresponding words on the page and point to them.

By getting him to do this, we are trying to help him develop a skill that many pre-school children develop on their own. They ask to have their favourite story read over and over again and get to know it by heart. They tell the story to themselves aloud, turning the pages at the right time to look at the accompanying pictures, and begin to match the words they are saying or hearing to the words on the page. Like most other people I have very little recollection of learning to read, but I do remember a time when I fixed my eye on the last word of each page of the story as my mother read to me. I tried to match it with the last word that she said before she turned the page.

Practising matching speech with print

Once the child has the idea of following the words in the book, he needs to practise with large print, simple, short sentences and few words to the page. Perhaps someone at home can read to him. A slightly older sister or a grandparent, maybe? The child can simply try to follow, or can repeat each phrase as he hears and matches it.

Multi-media reading software on a computer can be useful, as can listening to a taped story and trying to follow it in the book. (If we record the tape ourselves we can tap twice at the end of a page to help the child keep track in the book.) Rhymes, jingles, songs or hymns that he knows by heart can also be used. Write them or print them in large letters, and then show him that what he recites or sings matches what is on the paper. (I shall reword that: what he *should* be reciting or singing. If he has misunderstood or misheard the original, he may take a lot of convincing that his own often hilarious version is incorrect.)

Once we have started him off correctly matching the first few words with his finger, we can leave him to puzzle out for himself why he is still singing but has run out of words to point to, or why there are two words left on the page after he has recited the whole nursery rhyme. In this way we are encouraging him to learn how to break up heard English into lumps of sound called words, and to begin to recognise some of these words on the page.

What help would the child like?

During the time that we would normally allocate to hearing this particular child read, it may be well worth continuing the sound-sight matching we have just considered. Since he has made little progress in reading up to now, no matter who has tried to teach him, what about asking him what sort of help he finds useful?

Would he like us to read each page to him, several times if he wants, before he reads it to us? Or would he prefer us to do this in smaller lumps, paragraph by paragraph or sentence by sentence, before he reads? Or would he like us to read it with him, phrase by phrase, while he repeats it parrot-fashion, before he tries the page or paragraph on his own? We and he can learn as we go along. For example, if he hesitates longer than usual before repeating what we are reading, we might ask just, 'OK?' However, I have found that some children respond better if I suggest a range of possible answers: 'Do you want more time? Or would you like me to read it again, or do you want to stop now, or what?' I can only guess that it helps them to see more clearly what I am asking and what answer might be safe to give, especially if they are children who are not used to being consulted about anything.

Working sensitively and flexibly like this with a child may be particularly helpful at this early stage of his reading.

However, such an approach takes time. As our time is so limited, we need to think in terms of quality, not quantity, of reading experience. If we are in the habit of hearing weak readers read a few pages, we can, perhaps, decide to allocate this child the same amount of time while accepting that he may advance only a few sentences or paragraphs. How much he is moving on in his *learning* is what matters.

If we go along with his preferences, we still remain in charge. We make it very clear to him that he is the one doing the work, and that we expect him to apply himself. We expect him to practise and learn in whatever way he finds best, until he can read the paragraph or the page on his own, and can demonstrate the place he is at. Whether he is merely learning the words off by heart or is beginning to recognise them on the page does not matter at the moment. The one will gradually lead to the other anyway, provided we ensure that he looks at each word as he says it.

Learning to read by writing

Can we strengthen this child's understanding of reading by giving him more opportunity for quality writing? There are two distinct sources for this: one or two good sentences derived from his dictated words (see page 20, 'Not just for five-year-olds'), or one or two from the book, song, jingle, nursery rhyme or hymn that he has been practising. No guessing at spelling, no free writing, no copying off the board. This child needs to see and copy from something correct, meaningful to him, and under his hand. We practise it with him so that he knows what it says and can match the words he copies to the words he says.

Check what other basics he needs for reading

Context   Play the Context Game with him (see page 61) to make sure that he understands how to guess a word sensibly from context. In a very simple reading book with very few words to a sentence and a page, the sequence of pictures may give him more help than the words do.

Names of letters Check that he knows all the letters, both small and capital. If he is uncertain about the names of letters in isolation, can he at least recite the alphabet? If not, get someone in his family or at school to teach him alphabetic order. Learning alphabet songs as a class can help, too. Once he knows alphabetic order, he can practise letter names by saying the alphabet while pointing in turn to the printed letters.

Phonics Does he understand what phonics is all about? (See pages 43-46 of Chapter 3, Phonics, and in particular the first four suggested steps for action listed on page 44.) If he has apparently made some start in phonics, make sure that he realises that he can combine a little phonics with cues from context and syntax to help guess a word (see page 36, 'Using context, grammar and shape to help'). Not that I would explain in those words!

Shape A child who muddles 'little' with 'leg' or 'house' with 'hospital' is not using shape to help, although he may be using the initial letter. We need to increase his awareness of the length of a word and of letters sticking up or down. Check if there is any useful computer game for matching words with their blank shapes. Otherwise it is easy enough, though time-consuming, to produce work sheets or cards with words that have to be paired up with their outlined shapes. (See also the next paragraph on Handwriting.)

Handwriting Help him to see letters not in isolation but in relationship to each other and to the printed words on the page. He needs to get his letters correctly positioned and the right size relative to each other so that the shape of his written word more closely resembles the shape of a printed one. (See pages 102-105, 'Very uneven handwriting'.) Encourage him to say the word as he writes it.

Sight words Turn to the chapter on Sight words (page 67) for suggestions about how to build up a number of words he can recognise by sight. Keep a record of what he knows, and try to make sure he knows all the words in his reading book, preferably before starting it. We are trying to give him success and confidence. No matter what other words you teach him, make sure you remember to teach him essential words such as POISON, DANGER and TOILET. This is particularly important if the child is still virtually a non-reader but is of an age when he is likely to be out on his own. We consider his problem now.

Public signs and the older non-reader

A child old enough to be out and about on his own needs to be able to read all the various public signs he may come across. The following are in rough groups, some signs being included in more than one group.

TOILET, LAVATORY, PUBLIC CONVENIENCES, MEN, WOMEN, GENTLEMEN, GENTS, LADIES, BOYS, GIRLS, FREE, ENGAGED, HOT, COLD, NOT DRINKING WATER.

DANGER, WARNING, POISON, KEEP OUT, DEEP WATER, STOP, DON'T CROSS, DON'T TOUCH, DON'T DRINK, NOT DRINKING WATER.
(N.B. Explain that red is used to warn. A 10-year-old girl thought it was used to make signs and lights look pretty.)

WAY IN, WAY OUT, ENTRANCE, NO ENTRY, EXIT, NO EXIT, EMERGENCY EXIT, PUSH, PULL, BUS STOP, WAIT, CROSS, PEDESTRIANS.

CLOSED, SHUT, OPEN, PRIVATE, OFFICE, ENQUIRIES, INFORMATION, KEEP OUT, NO ENTRY, PRIVATE PROPERTY, KEEP OFF THE GRASS, NO CYCLING, ONE WAY.

An older child who is still virtually a non-reader has experienced so much failure that he is likely to be bored and resistant, so how are we going to teach him these public signs? Spare a moment to notice any examples visible in the classroom, around the main part of the school or in the neighbourhood. Pick about five of them, write or type them in large capital letters and give him a copy of them. Can he read them? If not, can he at least tell you what they mean? Show pleasure at any he knows, and record his success, with the date. Tell him what the others are. Can he spot the actual signs around the place?

It is very important that we show pleasure at any effort he makes, any success he achieves. It is as important to express that pleasure carefully – not 'Good lad' but 'Well done!' or 'That was a hard one to find!' (See pages 14-15 on praise.)

He needs to be able to identify the signs whether they are entirely in capital letters or in lower-case letters with an initial capital. So write or type both versions of the signs. Can he pair up the versions? If not, then here is an opportunity to get him to practise matching capitals and small letters. (See pages 105-107 of the Handwriting chapter.)

When he can identify all five signs, both in capitals and small letters, record his progress and the date visibly somewhere – on a chart, or with a star on a card, perhaps. Set him another five signs to learn and find. He could perhaps make a special 'Spot the Signs' book. He copies both versions of the signs into it, and then ticks each sign if and when he finds an example. To have a reminder like this of the progress he is making can be enormously reassuring and strengthening to a child who has experienced so much failure.

If necessary, ask another child to help him learn all the signs. And is there any appropriate software available?

Moving reading on

Analysing the child's word attack

Tape the child's reading and compare it with the book. Can you spot from his mistakes and hesitations which word-attack skills he is using, and which he needs to strengthen? (See pages 18, 36 and 60 for use of context and syntax; pages 18,

Chapter 6

26 and 57-58 for use of phonics; page 81 for noticing length and shape; page 67 for sight words; and pages 115-116 for the analysis of words.)

Is he reading for sense and managing to puzzle out difficult bits? If not, try him on an easier book with larger print and refer to the chapter on Comprehension (page 17).

Does he show marked strengths and weaknesses in his reading? The usual advice is to build on his strengths, but sometimes strengthening his weak side, however little, will pay off more. Is he, for example, good at recognising words by sight but very weak at using phonics? Teaching him to recognise more and more words by sight will help, of course, but I would rather try to move him forwards, however slightly, in phonics. For example, I would spend the time encouraging him to say words as he writes them (see pages 115-116 and 143-144) or getting him to practise blending without having to read (see page 54), or to recognise a rhyme (see page 41), or to use an initial sound in the Context Game (see page 61). The gain in his reading and confidence might be out of all proportion to the tiny improvement in his word-attack skills.

Feedback

Positive comment on his reading is going to help him particularly if we do not stop at 'Well done!' and its equivalents but go on to add what exactly we are pleased about. 'That was a word you did not know and you sounded it out.' 'You remembered that word from yesterday.' 'I enjoyed the way you read that funny bit.' (See page 14).

Personal space

One child may find it encouraging and comforting to sit or stand close to us when reading. Another may find it overwhelming or threatening because he feels it as an invasion of his personal space. We need to check how we ourselves are feeling at that moment, and certainly if the child seems tense or uncomfortable it is worth asking him if we are too close. Moving slightly away and to the side of the child can sometimes be very helpful.

Reading silently

Does he ever read silently? A beginner reader may think of reading only in terms of being read to by an adult or trying to read to an adult, and therefore always reads aloud even to himself. It can come as a surprise to him to find that he is allowed to read silently as well. I have come across parents who need to be reminded about this. They appear to be so keen for their child to learn to read well that they never leave him alone with a book but are always in there getting him to read it to them.

Maybe there is a lesson in that for us, too. Rather than expecting a child with reading problems always to read aloud to us, we might try occasionally allowing him the same amount of time as usual but getting him to read silently while we give him our silent attention and support. If he asks us what a word is, or what it means, we simply tell him without comment. Our aim is to take the pressure off him, to let him experience control of his own reading and enjoy some relaxed, uncomplicated human caring for a precious few minutes. Let me tell you about Sam in this context.

Sam

Sam was intensely disliked by teachers in his junior school. His name had only to be mentioned in the staff room for people to start swapping stories about his objectionable behaviour. The headmaster called me in to discuss Sam's reading. Although it was not much below average for his age, it was in marked contrast to the very high ability that he showed in maths and class discussions. We agreed that in view of this I would take Sam on his own for reading, giving him half an hour once a week for the next few weeks.

I was curious to meet him. He was quiet, expressionless and unforthcoming. He had brought a book with him which I listened to him reading for a few minutes. He read it badly, hesitating, stumbling, misreading whole phrases and having to correct them, but despite this I could not spot anything fundamentally amiss in his basic attack.

On an impulse I decided to do something I had never tried before. I told him that we would read the book together in silence, and that, as I was a faster reader than he was, it would be up to him to turn the page when he was ready.

So there we sat side by side reading in silence. When I had finished a page and was waiting for him to catch up, I used the time in trying to send positive feelings in his direction. I deliberately recalled happy moments in my own childhood, hide and seek, playing about in streams, rolling in hay, and digging on the beach.

At the end of the half hour I said quietly, 'Time to go now.' He closed his book, got up, walked to the door, turned, gave me a radiant smile, said, 'Thank you, Mrs Smith', and left.

Once a week for the next month we did exactly the same in silence. The only words I spoke were to tell him time was up, and he confined himself to that same radiant smile and thanks. The head told me that Sam's reading had taken off astoundingly, and his class teacher complained that the boy was still being a 'bloody nuisance' as he now always had his head in a book.

I had relied on my gut instinct, but who can tell what actually got Sam's reading going? Perhaps all he had needed was a quiet time to get together with a book on his own. I am grateful that I had an opportunity to give him that at least.

The child who still moves his lips

Does the child always move his lips when reading silently? Probably all of us do that and hear the words in our heads at times when what we are reading is heavy-going or we find it difficult to concentrate. Normally, however, it is better not to move our lips, and better still to get to the stage when we do not even hear the words in our head but somehow just 'think' them. Suggest to the child who moves his lips that he tries just to let go and allow his reading to happen. Putting his finger on his lips may remind him as he reads.

It is not a matter just of keeping our mouths still but of no longer hearing the words. Some years back I was with a group of children reading on their own when one of them exclaimed excitedly that something had just happened in his head. He said that his reading was different and easier and he did not hear it any more. A highly educated friend of mine would be envious of that boy as she still hears the words as she reads. The changeover seems to be at a subconscious level. I can only suggest relaxing and giving ourselves permission to let go of the sound in our heads. Going back to reading an extremely easy nursery book in silence may also do the trick for us as adults, because we will be able to take in the words and meaning at a glance.

Little or no support at home?

If a child is unlikely to get any help with his reading at home, can he have help from a parent volunteer or an older child? What about peer-tutoring (see page 90)? Can he use an interactive reading programme on the computer?

And what reading practice could he do at home? Perhaps he would take home a book he can read already and could read over and over again? Or an alphabet book with pictures and names? He could read this and copy the names. Or does he know a nursery rhyme, school song, hymn, pop song or advertising jingle? If we write or type some or all of the words in appropriately large letters, he can try to match the words on the page with what he can recite or sing. A child desperate to help himself will make good use of whatever time we spend like this.

Even though the people at home cannot or will not help him with his reading as such, they might be prepared to improve the lighting for him to read by if need be – an inexpensive desk lamp or bedside lamp or a higher wattage bulb in the ceiling fixture?

Reading badly to an audience

Is a child very bad at reading to an audience, even if he has practised the piece several times? He may be saying each word aloud as he gets to it, just as he probably did when he read his first reading book aloud to his teacher.

- Suggest that when reading aloud he reads each phrase or sentence first quickly to himself. This gives him a chance to make sure that he has read all the words correctly and understands what he is reading.

- Only then should he say the phrase or sentence aloud with expression, while looking up at the audience as much as possible.

- Reassure him that it is OK to keep the audience waiting while he pauses to read the next bit silently, and that he will speed up with practice. As he improves he will probably find that he can begin to read ahead while he is saying the previous bit aloud.

It helps to practise with an easy book and an uncritical audience. Has he got a little brother or sister he can read to? Or is there a non-reader in the school who would like a story read to him?

When reading progress slows down

Inadequate word-attack skills

A child with a good visual memory may run into difficulties when faced with an increasing range of reading material containing more and more words that he does not recognise by sight. He needs to employ phonic skills as well. Is it that he has not understood how to use the sounds he has been taught? (See page 43.) Or is it that he has not seen the point of using them because up to now he has managed fine without them? (See pages 43-45 and 57-58.) Or is it that he has been taught the sounds of the alphabet but phonics teaching stopped there, and he now needs to be taken through other phonic generalisations, *sh*, *ea*, *ow*, final *e* and so many more?

When language development and general knowledge need to be greater

A child may have adequate word-attack skills and make reasonable progress to start with but begin to struggle later on, maybe at a reading age of eight and a half or nine. This may not be through lack of phonics but because the child's vocabulary, command of English and limited experience and knowledge of life are not up to coping with the greater demands of the reading material he meets. Not only does he begin to lose comprehension of the whole passage that he is reading but also things get harder for him at word level. When he is not fully understanding what he is reading he is less likely to be able to predict the next word or to judge from the subsequent text whether the word was correct. For this reason alone he needs extra help with reading at school, particularly if he cannot count on getting any at home.

We need to pour language and understanding into him before we try getting any out. He has an even greater need than most to have stories and other books read to him long past the time when he might be considered capable of reading them himself. Also, rather than expecting him to read from 'cold', we would do better to read the story to him first and discuss it. This allows him to concentrate on the language and meaning before he tries reading it. When it is time for him to read, he may find it a help to hear each page or each paragraph again before he tries to read it on his own. Or we can read it again while he reads with us or repeats parrot-fashion after us if necessary. In other words, we can try a limited type of paired reading (see page 90) before he tries to read the passage on his own. This is similar to working with a child who is very weak on sight words. However, we are not trying so much to get him to link the word he hears with the word on the page as to make him familiar with the flow and meaning of a richer English than he is accustomed to. As his English improves, so will his comprehension and his ability to use context and syntax when reading.

Our time is so limited that we need to find additional ways of giving this child the reading help that he needs. Peer-tutoring may be the answer, particularly for older children, and we now consider this.

Peer-tutoring

Peer-tutoring, when one child helps another with his reading, may be well worth trying with older children of nine or ten or more who are significantly behind in reading. It falls into three types:

Shared reading Children work in pairs, taking it in turns to read, discussing the books, and helping each other over difficulties. This can be very successful, but not for the child whose language development is poor and who is lagging two or more years behind in reading. He is likely to respond better to the following two more structured models of peer-tutoring.

Paired reading Briefly, the child tutor reads simultaneously with the one being tutored unless the latter wants to read on his own. If the child pupil makes a mistake or pauses too long, the child tutor tells him the word, gets him to repeat it, and then starts reading with him again.

Pause, prompt and praise The child tutor hears the other one read. He does not rush in to help immediately there is a problem, but deliberately pauses to give the weak reader a chance to solve the problem on his own before prompting if necessary. He praises correct reading and success in solving problems.

Of the two more structured models, paired reading would be my choice for a child particularly weak in English. However, its success depends on whether we can find a child capable of tutoring well, as this way of tutoring is not easy.

Indeed, establishing peer-tutoring successfully is not at all easy. My brief, superficial description of shared reading, paired reading and 'Pause, prompt and praise' is inadequate to convey the breadth and depth of understanding, planning, organisation and tutoring actually necessary if peer-tutoring is to be as successful as research shows it can be. For further details of this interesting development in the teaching of reading I recommend Frank Merrett's book, *Improving Reading: A Teacher's Guide to Peer-Tutoring*, published by David Fulton Publishers, London.

Even though we may not be interested in setting up peer-tutoring, Mr Merrett's book contains much that could be very helpful when we ourselves hear children read. It also gives an account of experiments in which parents were helped to make paired reading with their children at home more effective and enjoyable.

The child we cannot help

The one time when we as teachers are definitely going to get nowhere is when the whole ethos of the family is against reading. Georgiana, George for short, seemed to be a very lucky little girl with doting parents, a lovely home with a swimming pool, several pets, skating at weekends, and exciting holidays. Yet her reading was well below what we would have expected, and try as I might I could not improve it at all. Nor could I identify her problem. All was revealed, however, at the parent-teacher interviews. I asked the parents if they read much themselves.

'No, never,' said this affluent father.

'Oh, I expect you do really,' I said encouragingly, thinking that so many people equate reading only with books.

He shook his head. 'I spend my time on DIY.'

I refused to give up. 'What about reading the instructions on the tins and packets you use?'

The mother burst into peals of laughter. 'If only he would! No, I'm the reader in the family. Mind you, I only read magazines, and not often.'

Chapter 6

She leant forward, looked over her shoulder for a moment and then added as if speaking about something indecent, 'I have heard that some people actually read in bed. I'm not like that!'

'Do you want George to learn to read?' I pursued.

They both nodded, and the mother said, 'Well, yes, but I wouldn't want it to become a habit!'

With a parental message like that, what hope of success has a teacher got?

Chapter Seven

Handwriting

'Remedial work often begins on day one.' This is the heading of a section in Dr Rosemary Sassoon's book *Handwriting: the way to teach it* (Leopard Learning, 1990). But what if not only days but some years have passed before a child with handwriting problems reaches us? Entrenched handwriting problems are not easy to tackle. This chapter suggests ways in which you might try doing so, but I recommend that you also study Dr Sassoon's excellent book.

Posture

A child should sit square to the working surface, with both feet on the ground.

If his chair and/or working surface is grossly out of proportion to his height he may sit very awkwardly, screwed right round, or with a leg under him, or with his head bent sideways practically on the desk. Battle with the problem of furniture, not with his attempt to alleviate severe discomfort. (If you win that battle, then help him change from a posture that may have become a habit.)

If the child is holding his pencil or pen so that it is blocking his view of his writing, he will have to bend over with his head on one side to see what he is doing. A better paper position and pen hold will solve this. See 'Paper position' (page 94).

If a child usually holds his head markedly to one side when writing and reading, he may, just may, have an eyesight problem of the kind not usually picked up in routine sight tests at school. An optometrist will be able to check.

When a child tries a new posture he may feel somehow exposed and vulnerable, and he may also find it difficult at first to control his pencil or pen. 'I can't write sitting like this. My writing has gone all funny.' We need to sell the child the idea that changing his posture will help him, and that, yes, it feels peculiar at the moment, but it will be worth it in the long run. We reinforce this by warmly praising any of his efforts to adopt a better habit. 'I see you are sitting straight at the table. Well done!' or 'Ah, you've remembered about your posture as you saw me coming. It isn't easy to remember. I'm glad you did.'

Paper position

Handwriting instruction books vary on the subject of paper position, but I strongly recommend the following.

For a right-hander Place the paper centrally or slightly over to the right. Slant it parallel to your writing arm.

For a left-hander Place the paper slightly over to the left so that the hand is just outside the body line at the start of writing. Slant the paper parallel to your writing arm.

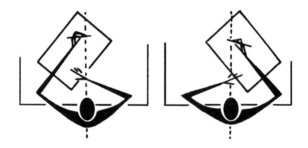

These positions help us to use the minimum physical effort for writing. Compared with a straight, square-on position, they allow a freer, more natural movement from the elbow, and left-handers will find that they no longer need to hook their hand right round. (See also page 96, 'Difficulties for left-handers'.)

Pencil hold

A good hold enables us to keep a straight wrist and use the top joints in our fingers and thumb rather than relying on movements from elbow and shoulder and, possibly, a bent wrist. For the great majority of people, both right-handed and left-handed, the most comfortable and efficient pencil or pen hold for writing is the conventional one as follows:

For right-handers A tripod/triangular grasp, that is, between thumb, forefinger and middle finger. The other two fingers rest on the paper, and the wrist is in a straight line with the forearm.

For left-handers As above, but possibly with the pencil held slightly farther up. (See 'Left-handers' overleaf.)

If the child cannot see how to hold the pencil, show him like this: place the pencil flat and pointing towards you at an angle of 90 degrees. Pick it up between thumb and forefinger only, holding it about 3 centimetres or 1.25 inches from the point. Now, swing the other end of the pencil over towards you (you may need to use your other hand to do this), and slip your middle finger underneath to support it. Get him to copy you.

A child may not have a strong enough grip to use this hold (and so persists in holding his pencil somehow else). Get him to strengthen his grip by frequently squeezing a plastic clothes peg. (Wooden ones are usually too strong.)

The tripod hold may not be suitable for a child with fingers of disproportionate length (such as an unusually short thumb or forefinger compared to the other fingers). Nor may it be suitable for a child with a damaged hand or some other physical difficulty. The important thing is that, if possible, he uses fine movements of his fingers and thumb or, failing that, his wrist, rather than large movements from elbow and shoulder. Like all of us, he needs to be able to move his pencil or pen with the minimum of effort and the maximum of fine control.

Ball-point pens work better if held more upright than other ink pens, and we need different holds for drawing and colouring with felt-tips, crayons and pencils.

Difficulties for left-handers

Left-handed hook Is the left-handed child curving his hand round the top of his writing? That is because his paper position or pencil hold was otherwise preventing him from seeing what he had just written. Show him the more comfortable left-handed paper position and pen hold described on pages 94-95. He will be able to see his writing if:

● he sits upright and with his head straight;
● he starts writing slightly to the left of his body line;
● he has his paper slanted slightly towards the right, parallel to his writing arm;
● he writes with a straight wrist;
● he holds his pen in a conventional tripod grasp – although he may prefer to hold it a little higher up than right-handers do.

Right-handed neighbour If a left-hander has to sit next to a right-hander, make sure the left-hander has the right-hander on his right so that their elbows do not get in each other's way.

Tension

A child may have an acceptable tripod pencil hold, but is he gripping the pencil so tightly that parts of his finger tips have gone white, or his forefinger is bent back unnaturally? Or is he pressing so hard that he is indenting the paper or even going right through it sometimes?

Maybe his pencil is too hard or his pen is scratchy and the ink will not flow. Try him with a soft dark pencil or a particularly smooth-flowing pen such as a fibre-tip or roller-ball one.

Is he very tense for some other reason? Show him how he can relax his muscles:

- by letting his arms hang down and go floppy, then shaking his wrists, hands and fingers;
- by circling his shoulders forwards and backwards to ease them.

Pencil hold – correcting a bad habit

A child (like the rest of us) can be very resistant to change. Defending his unhelpful pencil hold, he protests that 'Other teachers don't mind' or 'That's not what my Mum says.' Persevere. There is no reason for letting him get away with a bad habit that may affect the speed and ease of his writing for the rest of his life, and every reason to seek to improve the hold.

Will he learn better from another child? A slow learner, praised for his or her pencil hold, may be very helpful to another one. And pride may jerk a stubborn and opinionated high-flier into doing something about his terrible pencil hold if you ask a kind, less able child to teach him. Make sure that you thank the child helper warmly.

When a child tries a better pen hold, greet the change with quiet, warm approval. Support him through the first day or two by nurturing the new habit with praise and attention. Give him breaks from writing, as his fingers may be aching with all the new movements. Show him how to relax, as described above. Are we expecting the child to change then and there, and still complete several pages of work ready for Open Day tomorrow? Unrealistic. He needs time to get used to his new hold, so set him easier work targets.

In the early stages of changing to a better habit, the chances are that he will slip back when he is no longer thinking about it. Sympathise, and encourage him to keep checking, because once he is conscious of having slipped back to the old way, he can reassert the new hold. Persuade him that it is very important not to lash himself with thoughts

Chapter 7

like: 'Oh, wrong again! I'm never going to remember!' In
fact, he can be pleased with himself: 'Well done, me. I've
noticed! I'm getting there!'

This approach may sound strange or silly, but positive
self-talk *works*. Top athletes pay sports psychologists to teach
them positive imagery and self-talk. If we can get a child to
adopt the same positive reinforcement, who knows? He may
finish up at the Olympics, signing his autograph – with an
impeccable pen hold!

Not forming letters correctly

Is the child starting lower-case *d* from the top of the
ascender ('stick')? Is he writing *o* or *a* clockwise? Is he
starting lower-case *g*, *p* or *s* from the bottom? Does he start
lower-case *f* with a straight line down and then add a top
hook? If he is still forming some letters incorrectly like this
despite many efforts to teach him otherwise, we need to
examine how much effort he is putting into learning, and
what methods he is using to learn.

Make it clear to him that you *expect* him to form his
letters correctly. Explain that we all have to form our letters
the same way. (A child may think he has a choice.) Has he
got some special difficulty that we need to know about?
We so often forget to ask the child, and yet sometimes
his answer can take us straight to the problem and the
solution.

Demonstrate how to form a letter that he gets wrong.
Say its name, then talk about how to form it as you write it.
For example: '*d* (dee). Do a *c*, and then continue up, and
then do the stick straight down.' Get him to repeat your
actions and words.

Now get him to practise the letter in different ways, as
described on page 99. Aim to get him to maximise his
learning by using three or four senses simultaneously –
sight, hearing, touch and his sense of awareness of the
position of his body and the movement of his voluntary
muscles (his kinaesthetic or muscle sense).

Practising letter formation

Select one of his problem letters. We are going to take him back to the basic ways of learning it through various senses in combination. But first we make sure that he anchors this learning to something meaningful – so that he knows we are talking about the letter *f* for 'football' that he loves so much, or *b* for the 'bicycle' that he wants for Christmas.

Write the letter very large. Mark where he has to start and finish with different coloured dots, and show the direction with arrows. Tell him to trace over the letter first with his finger, again and again, saying the name of the letter, and talking himself through it if that helps. Then he is to trace it several times more using a pencil and tracing paper. If the parents will help, give them the model letter and ask them to make him go on practising at home.

Is he doing his best but still forming the letter in the wrong way? We widen the amount of information coming from his senses, particularly from touch and muscle movement. He needs to say the name of the letter while forming it over and over again:

- with huge movements of his hand and arm in the air;
- with a finger on sand, carpet or another rough material;
- with a finger on his knee or on the palm of his other hand.

Tell him to practise sometimes with his eyes closed so that he concentrates on what he is doing and feeling.

If the parents are willing to help, ask them to write the letter with a finger on his back, so that he feels it right through his body and then copies it in the air. (Make sure, of course, that the parents form the letter the right way themselves.)

Remember that, as the child practises, he needs to think about what the letter is and where he has met it before. When we get him to combine sight, hearing, touch, movement and understanding, we usually maximise his chance of learning and being able to recall (but see next paragraph). Mind you, he has got to be trying to learn, or we waste our time. Watch out for the child who sees no reason to learn because he is enjoying so much fuss and attention when the letters are not correct. Make it more rewarding to succeed. Give him your attention and approval when letters are correct, but play cool, firm and distant when they are not.

When a multi-sensory approach does not work

In theory, encouraging a child to synchronise input from three or four senses like this should work well, but it does not always do so in practice. A multi-sensory approach may not help a child if he does not make optimum use of each sense involved. For example, he may be looking carefully enough, but does not really take in at the same time what he hears and/or what he feels his muscles doing. In that case it may be worthwhile to change tactics and help him concentrate on a single sense.

I have already mentioned one way of concentrating on touch: keeping eyes shut while writing with a finger on knee, palm, sand or carpet.

The following is a suggestion for helping a child to concentrate first on sight and later on kinaesthetic sensations.

- Stand in front of the child. Tell him to hold his writing hand in front of him. Put your opposite hand out, in other words, your left and his right or vice versa. Your palms face each other (fingers pointing up), but not touching.

- Explain that you are going to form whatever letter it is, and that he is to move his hand at the same time like a mirror image, copying your hand but without touching it. Tell him that you are not going to talk because you want him to concentrate on what he is doing.

- Write the letter *in reverse* in the air (so it is the right way round for him) and get him to mirror it. Repeat this over and over again, remembering to close your hand and withdraw it slightly at the end of the letter each time. Speed up, but not so fast that he cannot keep up steadily.

- When he can do this and has a good rhythm going, tell him to shut his eyes while still practising the letter. (This focuses his mind on the sensation from his muscles and the position of his arm and hand in space.)

- If he begins to falter, tell him to open his eyes and mirror you some more before trying again with his eyes shut.

The child who is not learning

If children are expected to practise letter formation by writing rows of each letter, we need to move around the class keeping a close eye on how this is being done. Watch out for the child who is not learning. Told to practise a line of *d*s, for example, he decides to do a row of *c*s first and then go back to add the sticks, or maybe he does the sticks first and then adds the *c*s. He has missed the point. He has not learnt to form letter *d*. Maybe we have not explained the importance of the right formation and that we are not punishing him but trying to establish a new habit. Or is he deliberately not cooperating with the adults in his life? If so, peer pressure may help, especially if you have the whole class working towards the goal that everyone gets all the letter formations right.

C group letters

If a child starts his letter *c* at a 12 o'clock position and immediately curves round to 11 o'clock, it adversely affects the shape of his *a*, *d*, *g*, *q* and possibly his figure *9*. Teach him to start *c* (and these related letters) either with a curve from one o'clock or two o'clock back up to twelve o'clock, or with a short straight movement from right to left – depending on which model alphabet is being taught. Once he does this he should have no difficulty in closing these *c* group letters, and his handwriting will improve.

Note that someone who is right-handed needs to make a push stroke at the beginning of the *c*, while the left-hander just has to pull. Pushing the pen or pencil away from us is harder than pulling it towards us. A right-handed child with very poor hand control may need special understanding and extra practice to achieve well-shaped letters in this group – but it is well worth persevering.

Lower-case *f* and *t*

Does his *f* look like a capital *S* crossed through the middle? Horrible! He has not noticed that *f* is actually a long straight letter that starts with a curve, then goes straight down to the line and finishes there, or carries on below the line to finish with another curve like a *g*. He has not noticed, either, that the crossbar does not come in the middle but higher up, horizontal with the top of a lower-case *o*. With a curved tail below the line, *f* becomes the longest letter, and a very beautiful one when written well. If we can get the child to see and understand this letter, we may start him on the way to enjoying handwriting.

And what does he do with his small *t*? Has he not yet noticed that it is not as high as other tall letters? And what about the crossbar? Does his lower-case *t* look like a plus sign or else like a signpost showing a road going off to the right? He has not noticed that *t*'s crossbar, like that of *f*, is short and level with the top of a lower-case *o* or *e*. Nor has he noticed that it starts just slightly to the left of the upright.

These are examples of small details that can make or mar a person's handwriting.

Very uneven handwriting

The relative position of letters

Help the child to concentrate on this single issue by removing the need to write.

- You need plastic lower-case ('small') letters. (Cheap sets of these are sometimes ill-proportioned. Try to borrow a good-quality set from the infant school.) You also need a strip of paper more than long enough for all the letters of the alphabet placed side by side. Sheets of A4 taped together lengthways will do.

● Right along the centre of the strip, using a thick pen, draw two parallel lines, just wide enough apart for the plastic *o*, *a* or *e* to fit in the white space between them.

● Show the child how to put this kind of letter (the ones without sticks and tails) exactly between the lines.

● Show him how sticks and tails of other letters protrude above or below the lines.

● Get the child to place all the letters correctly himself, in any order. (Do not complicate the issue by demanding alphabetic order at the moment.)

● Get him to make simple words that he can read – but not his name unless the set of plastic letters includes capitals of proportionate size.

The relative size of letters

A child may write very unevenly long after you judge him to have gained sufficient maturity and control of his writing to do something about it. Try these steps:

● Ensure he understands how to position plastic letters on parallel lines, as explained above.

● Estimate his preferred size of writing from several samples of his work. Judge usually from the average height of his lower-case *o*, but refer to his *a*, *e* and *c* as well if the size of his *o* varies wildly. (Capitals are often not a reliable guide.)

- Draw parallel lines on plain paper, the right width apart to fit his small *o* as estimated above.

- Show him how to position his written letters in the lines, with sticks and tails protruding, as he positioned the plastic letters. Point out that he has to form the main body of his letters (for example, the 'tummy' of *b*) to meet both lines exactly. Use the plastic letters to show this.

- Add a line above and a line below his pair of lines, the same distance apart (that is, one *o*'s width from them). Show him that his sticks and tails (ascenders and descenders) have to meet these outer lines but not protrude beyond them.

- Point out that *t* is the exception. It does not touch the top line but sticks up only just above a 'body' letter like *o*.

- Point out that the crossbars of *t* and *f* always lie along the line marking the top of *o*. Depending on what script the school uses, the *f* finishes on the baseline or has a curved tail touching the bottom line.

- Show him that capital letters should all touch the top line and 'stand' on the third line down, the baseline, with nothing protruding beyond those lines, except possibly for the tail of *Q*.

- Show him how to write figures (numbers) like capital letters, touching the top line and standing on the baseline.

Letters in the script taught in your school may differ from the above proportions. Remember, however, that we are considering a child with marked difficulties over handwriting.

The simpler we make it for him the better. Small deviations from the school script may help him to understand handwriting better and write more evenly. For example, if his cursive *s* is hideous and as large as a capital letter, consider allowing him to use an infant *s*. This may considerably improve the appearance of his handwriting.

A child who has been writing unevenly will need a lot of practice to improve. I suggest you rule up a whole sheet with sets of four lines of the size you have established as appropriate for his writing and then make several photocopies. Give him an example of the alphabet and his name written to fit these lines. This example is best stuck to card so that he can keep it for reference.

Once the child is able to alter the size of his writing without much difficulty, he can use paper with printed double or quadruple lines. Discarded computer paper with tramlines can be useful for practice.

Note that if a child has a great problem seeing which line he has to use, it could be that he has an eyesight problem. An optometrist can check for this. Not all eyesight problems are picked up in routine tests at school.

Capital letters and small ones

Confusing capitals with lower-case letters

If a child is muddled about capitals and lower-case letters he needs to have an alphabet of capitals and small letters that he can constantly refer to. Draw the writing baseline in pencil, and preferably the other three lines as well so that he understands the relative position of the pairs of letters. (See preceding section.)

We can give him practice changing a passage from lower-case to capitals or vice versa (not forgetting that sentences and proper nouns have to start with a capital). We can also have him type something in lower-case, which of course entails finding the equivalent capital letter on the keyboard. However, ultimately the child just has to start applying his mind to getting the case correct. Having to write a corrected word or sentence once or twice in best handwriting every time there is a mistake may help – help, not punish.

Confusing small/lower-case with small/little

A child can get muddled when we talk about 'small letters' when we mean lower-case ones. He confuses small meaning tiny with small meaning not capital. The school may think to get round the problem by always calling letters upper-case and lower-case, or majuscules and minuscules. However, as the child is likely to hear people at home calling them capitals and smalls, or even big ones and small ones, the muddle may remain. He may, for example, have some idea that capitals have to be enormous because they are not 'small'.

We can clarify things for the class in a practical exercise. Write a capital letter on the board, choosing a letter that has a different lower-case form, e.g. *A*, *B*, *D*, *E*, *F*, *G* or *H* but not *C*, *O*, *P* or *V*. Get the children to agree that it is a capital, and then ask one of them to come up and write its 'small' letter next to it and in proportion, so that we now have on the board, for example, *Aa* or *Bb*. Note that we are deliberately still using 'capital' and 'small' for the purposes of this lesson. They are the terms that caused confusion in the first place, and we are going to sort out things for the children with these words that they are used to.

Write another capital but a completely different size, very small or very large, and get a child to add the equivalent 'small' letter. Stick to letters that have a different lower-case form. Point out that there are large 'small' letters and small 'small' letters, and that capitals can be large or very small, and that their small letters have to be in proportion.

Then write lower-case letters and have the children add the corresponding capitals. After that sometimes write a lower-case letter, sometimes a capital, and let the children decide which form they need to add.

Repeat, but this time using letters that have the same shape whether capital or small (*C*, *O*, *P*, *V* and possibly others depending on the script used in the school). We can show that these can be capitals or 'small' ones, and that the only way of telling is to compare them with another letter. Write one of these letters, any size, and ask a child to come up and write a letter on one side of it or the other to show whether the original letter is a capital or a small (lower-case) one. For example, just by adding another letter, the child can make **O** lower-case (e.g. **on** or **no** or **No**) or a capital (e.g. **On** or **NO** or **ON**). We demonstrate other letters like this, including the plain vertical line that may be a lower-case **L** or a capital **i** (or a number **1**). We can also demonstrate the ambiguity of some poorly written forms of **F**, **M**, **W**, and the need for dotting **i** and **j**.

Block capitals

Block capitals are capitals all the same height, separate from each other and without serifs and fancy bits of our own. Make sure an older child can write them evenly. He will need them for form-filling. A child may find it difficult not only to get them all the same height but also to write them smaller than usual.

Provide a sample alphabet written in block capitals for him to copy on plain paper. Get him to start by writing just the capital **A**, but smaller than his usual writing. Extend lines from the top and bottom of this **A**, parallel across the paper, to guide the rest of his block capitals.

Once he can manage to write the alphabet that size, using clear block capitals, he can practise his full name, date of birth and address. He can then go on to practise writing them smaller and smaller, first still using two guide lines and then just one. For fun, he can try writing his details in smaller and smaller rectangles or on lines of varying lengths. Later in his life it will be for real.

Incidentally, be prepared to teach more than block capitals. He may not know how to spell his middle names if he has any, nor know his address, let alone his date of birth. (If we know that some of the class are living in temporary accommodation or a refuge, we can get all the class to give the school address.)

Chapter 7

Problems learning joined-up writing

A child can become thoroughly confused over joining letters, especially if he has not fully understood and practised the basic letter forms. See if any of the following will help.

● Provide simple words written in very large joined-up writing. Make the basic letters black and the joining strokes in another colour. Use coloured dots to show where to start, and arrows to mark the direction where necessary.

● Get him to trace over the writing again and again, first practising with his finger and then with a pencil and tracing paper. *Tell him to say the name of each letter as he writes it.* This ensures that he is not just practising a meaningless shape but at least links it to the letter name. Saying the name also increases his chance of recalling the letter's formation because he adds auditory and articulatory input to the activity. He continues to practise in various ways as necessary until he can write the words correctly without tracing them. See pages 98-102, 'Not forming letters correctly', for full details of learning methods.

● Once he has mastered these words, give him a sheet of large unjoined writing and tell him to use a coloured pen to put in joins where appropriate. Explain if necessary that joining every letter every time does not work. It is too slow and makes for muddles. He has to learn the rules.

● Try talking him through what you are doing as you write something. For example, you are writing the word 'dog'. '... Now, I've finished the *d* down on the line. But the next letter is *o* so I don't bother to take my pen off. Instead I move it up and curve it to where I am going to start the *o*. ...' etc. (Something like that. Everyone has their own style.)

- Explain that the joined-up form of letters is no better nor more grown-up than the basic form he has already learned, just quicker to use in some places. For example, the joined-up *s* taught in your school may not retain much of the shape of the basic *s* and he may imagine that it is a very special new letter he always has to write. But his writing may be clearer if he uses an ordinary basic *s* at the start of a word or for *ss*.

- Provide him with double or quadruple lines so that he does not lose the even size of his writing.

Atrocious handwriting

Identifying the problem

If a child reaches you with atrocious handwriting without an obvious reason such as poor hand control, assess the problem. Read his records (if and when they arrive), and *watch him as he writes something*. Note his posture, paper position, pencil hold, tension, letter formation, size and evenness of writing, joins and speed. Deal with particular problems revealed as suggested in the earlier sections of this chapter. That may sound easy, but requires tremendous commitment, patience and determination from us, I know.

Uncovering poor spelling

Is the child trying to cover up his poor spelling by deliberately making his writing extremely small or practically illegible? No one likes his mistakes in full view, so empathise with him, promise to help him with his spelling problems, and try to persuade him to deal with his handwriting as a separate issue. Show that you understand that he is likely to feel embarrassed and vulnerable if he writes larger and more clearly. Praise his courage when he manages to do so, and praise what you can of his changed writing. *Make no reference at all to any spelling mistakes.* If he refers to them himself, reassure him that it is OK, and that you are concentrating on his handwriting at the moment.

In general

Expect the child to improve his writing, tell him so, and warmly acknowledge any effort to comply. (See page 97 for suggestions for correcting a bad habit.) However, we cannot expect him to correct everything at once. Limit the task. Set him small, attainable goals so that he can experience success and praise. For example, ask for one word or line written well, or every letter *a* in one page of writing correctly formed, or correct posture and pen hold maintained for three minutes of writing. Furthermore, give the child a chance to repeat and enjoy this level of success for two or three days or longer before setting him the next challenge, unless, of course, he asks for it earlier.

Explain that he has no choice over letter formation and relative size of letters, and little choice over whether letters join or not. We all need to conform if we are to communicate efficiently. However, within these limits, consider giving an older child a slight choice over some letters. Allowing him some individuality may motivate him if, at present, he feels mutinous and in a straitjacket over handwriting. Suggestions: a slight flourish on the final letter of his name or at the end of a sentence (e.g. on the crossbar of *f* or *t*, or the end of *k* or *w*). Or allow him to use a basic *s* or basic *r* if he is finding it difficult to write them well in the form required in the school script. Or teach him a Greek letter *e*.

As always, praise where you can. Does he at least form his *o* anticlockwise, or cross his *f* at the right height? Point out or tick or circle the good examples of letters and words he has written and express specific pleasure: 'A well-closed *a*', or 'Well-joined letters' or 'How nice to see a beautiful capital *W*.'

Be wise for the child and persevere with him. We cannot expect him to appreciate the long-term importance of fast, fluent, legible handwriting, but we know how valuable it is. A child deserves our insistence that he works to a high standard (just as he deserves our warm approval when he does so). Why deny him the very personal pleasure of good handwriting?

Chapter Eight

Copying and self-checking it

In this chapter we consider the problems a child may have in copying accurately, whether his own dictated work, the title of a book, words needed for a topic on space, or a poem in a handwriting lesson. We look at various causes of error and at ways of improving copying skills, leading not only to greater accuracy but to improvements in reading and spelling generally. We also consider how to teach a child to check his own copying for mistakes.

Problems when copying from a near position

Is the reading level too high?

Is what he has to copy so far above his reading ability that he has little or no idea of the subject matter, cannot read most of the words and is reduced to copying letter by letter? He needs to be able to read and understand the words and the passage if he is to have a chance to improve his spelling and begin to understand punctuation and the forms of English. Being made to copy meaningless strings of letters can only teach him that school is boring.

We limit a child's copying to the level he can cope with. If he can barely read anything at all, then he is at the level of copying a word with an identifying picture, or a line from his first reading book, or a phrase he has dictated that we have written under a picture he has drawn. We read the words for him, if necessary several times, getting him to repeat them and to point to them with his finger. If he can do this, we know that he can match a heard word with a printed one. (For the child who cannot match spoken words with printed ones, see page 77).

Printed pictures of objects may be obvious to us but we still need to read the accompanying words with him, or we run the risk of his copying the word 'rat' while saying 'mouse' to himself. We do not allow him to start copying until we are reasonably sure that he will know each word as he writes it. Afterwards we can get him to read back what he has copied. Reading and writing go closely hand in hand at this level.

Even copying from another piece of paper or book may be too hard for someone with great problems, so be prepared if need be to write the words in his exercise book so that he can copy them immediately underneath.

Has he eyesight problems?

Is he failing to distinguish between visually similar letters? For example, has he written *u* instead of *a*, or *o* instead of *e*? Does he keep glancing at what he is copying, far more often than seems necessary? Does he hold his head on one side, or turn it so that he is not square on to what he is looking at? An optometrist will be able to check for the type of eyesight problems that are not picked up in an ordinary school eye test. Or is it that he has glasses but is not wearing them, or is wearing glasses so filthy or scratched that he can barely see through them?

Or is it just that the writing or printing is too small for someone of his reading age, so that he has difficulty in distinguishing between small, visually similar letters? Smaller print may also mean that he is confronted with printed forms of *a*, *g*, *k* and *y* that he may not have learnt yet. Try larger print or handwriting.

Is the original indecipherable?

How clear is the original he is trying to copy? Is it very poorly reproduced, faint, smudged, on poor paper? This makes reading and copying so difficult for all but the best readers that I suggest you rethink the lesson and/or arrange for the weakest to do something more within their capabilities.

If handwritten, is the original written precisely enough for a weak reader? If, for example, we rarely bother to close the top of our lower-case *a*, is it really surprising if he copies it as *u*?

And what about joined-up writing? Have all the class learnt it by now? Watch out in particular for any new child who may not have learnt joined-up writing in his previous school. I have known teachers leave a child to sink or swim, on the grounds that he *ought* to have been taught it by that age. Even a high-flier may have a terrible struggle trying to read and copy this strange new handwriting. Parents and children themselves have told me with great feeling years later what an ordeal and setback this was. It is our responsibility to deal with the child's problem. Provide him with the appropriate handwriting practice book – begging one from lower down the school chain if necessary – and find time to help and encourage him to learn from it, or get someone else to help him do so. The child deserves to feel understood and valued as he struggles with a problem not of his own making.

Copying just letter by letter?

By watching him as he copies we can see if he is still copying only letter by letter as he would have done when he started school. For example, Patrick was reading at about a seven-year-old level, but I noticed that he copied only one or two letters at a time. He copied down the 'ha' of 'had' and then looked again at the original to see what came next. On questioning him I found that it had never occurred to him to read the words. He agreed, with surprise, that, yes, of course he could have written 'had' in one go if he had realised what it was. He immediately and with enthusiasm set about copying two or three easy words at a time.

Copying just shape by shape?

I came across Kev. He appeared to be a much weaker reader than Patrick, and was in deeper difficulty. I could see that he, too, was copying one letter at a time, but very slowly, and sometimes looking at it again. This could have indicated an eyesight problem. A child who looks again and again at what he is copying may need to have his sight checked by an optometrist. However, Kev's problem turned out to be different.

Chapter 8

I asked Kev, as I had asked Patrick, if he would mind sharing with me what went on in his head as he copied. I pointed to an *m*, and asked him what he did when he copied it – did he say 'mmm' to himself or 'em' or what?

Kev looked blank. I probed again very gently. 'It would be a great help to me if you could tell me what happens when you copy. When you look and then start copying, what do you say to yourself? What do you think about?'

Kev struggled to explain. It became clear that he had been just copying shapes one by one without naming them to himself at all. (Compare Melanie's difficulties, reported on page 151 of Chapter 9, Spelling.)

Does a child like this still not know the names and/or sounds of letters, let alone the words, despite the school's efforts to teach them? If so, this task of copying is totally meaningless and unhelpful. He needs our urgent attention and a proper assessment of his needs. Or is it that the child does now know the names and sounds of letters but is persisting in an earlier habit like Patrick, because it has not occurred to him to use his developing knowledge?

By the way, I am deeply moved when a child like Kev risks telling me what he is thinking as he copies. It takes courage when one is a long way behind the rest of the class and has probably been battered throughout childhood by 'Oh, don't be such a fool!', 'Trust you to do a stupid thing like that' and 'How many times have I told you ...'.

Not reading through first?

Is a child making copying mistakes because he begins to copy without the slightest idea what the sentence, let alone the whole thing, is about? We encourage him to glance through the whole text before starting, and then to tackle one sentence at a time, reading the whole of it carefully this time, before copying it word by word, or phrase by phrase. If he does not read ahead before copying, the text unfolds for him only letter by letter, or, at best, word by isolated word, and the task is made meaningless. But if he understands what he is copying he has an opportunity to improve his knowledge of syntax, spelling and the use of punctuation, and thus also indirectly to improve his reading. For example, he may begin to think about inverted commas or to notice when 'too' is used rather than 'to', or he may discover that what he had always thought of as 'wuns poner' is actually 'Once upon a'.

Not analysing the word?

Does he think carefully about the word he is about to copy? Or does he merely glance at it and quickly start writing?

If a child is very bad at copying, unobtrusively observe him doing it. I have come across children who read a word quickly, start writing it down, and then struggle to spell it. They hesitate, look out of the window or up at the ceiling for inspiration, and then write down their version which is often incorrect. Why does it not occur to these children to look back at the original? I do not know. Some perhaps do not yet see any connection between reading a word and spelling it, and have got the two activities in separate compartments in their minds. Some may have made the same mistake as Nathaniel. A very intelligent boy, Nathaniel, whose reading difficulties probably arose from emotional factors at home, was under the impression that copying was a spelling test, and that he was not allowed to copy the spelling from the original but had to work it out for himself.

We need to teach children who are poor at copying like this to read the word – in other words, identify it – and then to look carefully at how it is spelt. Does it have a double letter, or a silent one, or is it spelt in a peculiar way? Has it got more than one syllable? Are those syllables spelt phonically? How is the indeterminate sound of its end spelt (e.g. animal, camel, little, symbol, awful) and what is the best way of remembering that? Only after they feel on top of the spelling should they look away from the original and start to copy it.

Not saying the word?

Is he not using sound to help him learn, to help him associate what he is seeing with what he is writing? All he needs to do is to say the word under his breath, stretching it out to synchronise with the writing of it. Sometimes, he may prefer to spell out the word, mouthing the letters to himself as he writes them and then saying the complete word. He should mouth the words or letters distinctly, moving his lips clearly, as this helps him to remember – and to concentrate.

With a phonically regular word like 'chimpanzee' he can say the syllables as he writes them.

With an irregular word like 'yacht' he has choices:

- He can spell it out and then say 'yacht' (yot) to himself.
- He can say 'yuh-o-tuh' to himself as he writes 'y-ach-t', and pay attention to the mismatch.
- He can say it as it looks (rhyming with 'matched' and 'hatched') and remember it that way.

It does not matter which way he chooses. The important thing is that he actively uses his auditory sense and the movements of his mouth and tongue to help him with its spelling.

Not checking as he goes?

Does he not bother to check difficult words after he has copied them? He needs to get into the habit of checking long words, unfamiliar names, strings of numbers, dates and so on, as he goes along. Checking them immediately after writing them can save trouble later, and he will be practising unfamiliar spellings correctly from the start. Suppose he does not take the opportunity when copying to notice that 'Parliament' has an *a* after the *i*. Having written it once incorrectly, he may continue to do so for years until someone corrects his spelling – if they ever do.

Not organising his working space?

Has he organised himself for copying? Has he got the original conveniently near, or is he peering at it from a distance across a pile of books while trying to write with his arm resting on his pencil case?

It may never have occurred to him that he can control his working space. We show him that he could decide to put his pencil case and books away for the time being, or at least stack them neatly to one side. We also tell him to bring the original he has to copy as near as possible to his page. When appropriate, he can tuck the bottom half of it under his exercise book, or fold the exercise book back on itself.

Having explained and demonstrated, it is important that we insist that all the children clear their working space properly before starting to write. We want it to become a good working habit.

Not using his finger?

Does he forget to keep a finger on the original to mark where he has got to? A finger there helps him to focus his eyes and his mind on the word, and to find his place again after copying a bit. It also prevents him from leaving a whole chunk out, or duplicating it, which is easy enough to do when he looks to find his place again and does not realise that he is picking up at the same word in a different part of the passage.

Additional problems when copying from the board

Even a child who has no problem copying from an original under his hand may run into difficulties when trying to copy from a distance.

Is the writing legible?

Is the writing big and clear enough for a child of his reading age when he is sitting at a distance? Try writing larger.

Are you expecting him to copy from a filthy, pock-marked board? Is your writing barely discernible because your pen is beginning to run out? He does not need such an unhelpful challenge. Give him something else to do.

Can he see from where he is sitting?

Is the light shining on the board from where the child is sitting? Or is the sun in his eyes and the board in shadow, so that his eyes are having to adjust every few moments from light to dark and back again? Intolerable working conditions. Do something about it.

Is he sitting with his back to the board so that he has to keep swivelling round while copying? A child may forget what he has seen in the time it takes him to turn round and write it. It may be the school policy to have everyone sitting round tables, but in this instance it results again in intolerable working conditions. Do something about it.

He manages close copying, but can he see all right from a distance? Does he need his sight checked? Or has he had it checked already and has been given glasses for distance work, although no one has informed us, and he has probably left his glasses at home deliberately anyway? Is he supposed to be sitting near the board? Have we got him sitting on the left of the board although his records state that the sight in his right eye is very poor? *Have we read his records?*

Copying handicaps

Patrick could not see the board at all past a stack of maths equipment, and so was reduced to trying to copy from the boy next to him, although that boy was enjoying trying to stop him from doing so.

David, on the other hand, was expected to get up from his seat, take several steps round a huge and very beautiful arrangement of indoor plants, look at the board and then dash back each time before he forgot what he was copying.

Does he omit words?

Does he leave out words or even great chunks of text? It is probably because he keeps losing his place. He cannot put his finger on the board, as he can on a page, to mark the place he has reached. When he looks up from writing he does not always know where on the board he has got to. He has just copied 'very', so he finds 'very' on the board and carries on, but the 'very' he has found may be several lines farther on (or back) from the 'very' he needs.

Tell him that he has got the right idea about finding his place on the board, but that he needs to look not for just the last word that he copied but for the last several words. Mouthing the words under his breath will help him concentrate. He needs to keep repeating them until he finds the matching words on the board and can carry on copying from there. For example:

Part of what is on the board to be copied:

Volcanic soil is very rich in chemicals needed by plants, so it is good for growing crops.

He has copied as far as: 'Volcanic soil is very rich'. He now keeps repeating the last words he has written until he finds them on the board again. '... is very rich ... is very rich ... Ah! Here we are! ... Volcanic soil is very rich *in chemicals*'.

He copies 'in chemicals', and then repeats and searches in the same way: 'rich in chemicals ... rich in chemicals ... Ah! rich in chemicals *needed by plants comma*.' He writes 'needed by plants,'.

We can suggest two quick additional checks for him to do if he tends to leave out chunks of text. If he has copied a poem, he can count the lines and verses to check that he has got the same number. If long text, has he got the same number of paragraphs, or all the notes from a-f or 1-6?

Is he relying too much on just looking?

Is he making more small mistakes than when he was copying from a near position? He may be relying too much just on visual memory. By the time he has transferred his gaze from the board to his piece of paper he may be losing the image. He needs to analyse the words he is about to copy more thoroughly *before he looks away*. (See page 115, 'Not analysing the word?') Make sure that he is sitting facing the board.

Self-checking what he has copied

Expect children to check their work

One of our important long-term aims is to teach the child how to work independently to high standards, and this includes how to check something that he has copied. Does he leave all the checking to us at present? Almost certainly if we never expect him to do any.

Chris's school (below) is unfortunately not the only secondary school faced with a gargantuan struggle to pull up the standards of pupils of whom not sufficient was expected earlier in their school life. In my opinion, we let children down if we do not teach them to check their own work as far as they are able, and to do this before handing their work in for us to check in turn. Teaching a young child with literacy problems how to check will improve his spelling and his awareness of such necessities as capital letters and punctuation marks which he has perhaps blithely ignored up to now. It will strengthen his reading and writing in general.

One man against the tide

Chris, head of a science department in a big comprehensive school, told me in 1996 that he had given up trying to get his senior pupils to check their work. Most of them were expecting to go on to college or university, yet he said that they were handing in work riddled with careless mistakes. In all their years at school they had never checked their work and saw no reason why they should start doing so now.

Too much to expect?

If some schools have been so reluctant to expect even their high-achievers to check their own work, is it absurd to ask such practices of a young child who is struggling already? In my opinion, not at all, provided that, as usual, we set him a task well within his ability. Remember, all we are going to teach him is to check his own copying against the original. This is no punitive exercise against sloppy work, but a chance to help a child focus on things he has not quite mastered, whether it be the difference between a capital *S* and a small one, the formation of *g*, or that 'feild' does not spell 'field'.

How do you like checking your own work? Boring? Something you avoid doing? Then you have good reason for doing your best to make checking an exciting challenge for the child and a rewarding one when he succeeds. 'Wow, you found it! That was quick. Well done!' Forget that he made the mistake in the first place. Concentrate on encouraging good self-checking. Point out that checking is like doing 'Spot the Difference' puzzles. When he finds that he can get plenty of ticks and praise, he may love doing it.

The right level to set

Is the child's copying peppered with mistakes? Evidently whatever he tried to copy was too hard for him. Expecting him to find and correct all these mistakes is not a good idea. Forget it. He needed something easier to copy. Next time he has to copy anything, give him a shorter, easier piece, well within his reading ability, level of handwriting and span of concentration. (See pages 111-119.)

Our aim is to get him to copy at a level where he can achieve 100 per cent accuracy most times, and is making only an occasional mistake. We can then praise his accuracy (which may be a novel experience for him), and show great pleasure when he learns to spot the odd one or two mistakes. This may mean having to take him back to copying a single sentence or a single word, and perhaps even to copying it on the same piece of paper, immediately under the original.

Go through the child's copied work carefully looking for mistakes, but do not mark them. Instead, indicate next to the appropriate line that there is one mistake or more that he has to find and correct. If necessary, make it simpler than that by telling him what kind of mistake he is looking for – a capital letter instead of a small one, a letter written the wrong way round, one word misspelt, or some punctuation mark that he has missed. Remind the child not just to reread the line but to check against the original as well.

Reluctant to correct mistakes?

What if he appears to have known perfectly well about his mistakes before he handed in his work? What was his difficulty that he did not put them right? Is he not sure that he is allowed to correct them? Is he feeling that the job is too hard for him and he wants to leave it to us? Have we set him a task that is too long for his concentration span? Have we gone through the basic checklist that needs always to be at the back of our minds (see page 27)?

But is it that he is so proud of the neat appearance of his work that he resists any idea of 'spoiling' it by corrections? Is he the sort of child who has to be 'perfect' or else goes to pieces? Are we clear about what we are trying to teach? If the work at issue is just everyday class work, are we over-emphasising the importance of appearance at the expense of accuracy? Or is the problem with the child and/or his parents? Is there anything we can do to help him feel more accepted and valued as a person even when he makes mistakes?

Examples of the mistakes scribes made in ancient manuscripts, and how they corrected them, may interest him. Show him how he himself can use a caret (the omission mark that looks like an upside down *v* or *y*), and/or a note in the margin, or an asterisk. Discuss which way of correcting would be appropriate for his mistake. Try a demonstrating way of talking that conveys that we all make mistakes: 'Oh, bad luck! Now, when I make that sort of mistake I usually ... or I might decide to ...'.

As he finds mistakes so difficult to live with, we need to be ready to accept his feelings, and praise in a way that may help him. 'Well done. I like the way you have neatly corrected that bit.' (The equivalent of: 'You may have knocked over the milk bottle, but you have done a grand job of clearing it up.')

Getting down to checking carefully

What if he cannot spot even the most obvious mistake? He may be just reading in the usual way and not *actively* looking for mistakes. Or he may have read through but not gone on to compare his copy with the original. Also point out that, if there is something we are always reminding him about – forgetting to use a capital after a full stop, perhaps – it is sensible to look out specially for that.

To check his copying very carefully he needs to compare the original with his copy, word by word, or even get down to comparing each single letter, punctuation mark and space, using a finger on the original and another on his copy. He should ask himself what exactly he is looking at on the original, and whether he has got that on his copy. Mouthing what he is comparing will help him concentrate on this difficult job.

Original: *Something was different.*

His copy: *Something was difficult.*

Checking: '*Something* ... have I got *Something*? Yes. *was* ... have I got *was*? Yes. *different* ... have I got *different*? Oops, no, I've put *difficult.*'

Checking from a distance is harder because the child cannot put his finger on the original. He needs to repeat a few earlier words just as he did when he copied from the board.

Original: *The Greeks used to think that pieces of iron*

His copy: *The Greeks used to think that pieces iron*

He checks: '*The Greeks* ... have I got *The Greeks*? Yes, I have. *The Greeks used to think* ... Have I got *used to think*? Yes. *used to think that pieces of iron* ... Have I got *that pieces of iron*? ... Oh, I see, I've left out *of.*'

Still not finding all mistakes?

Is he still not finding all his mistakes? Are we expecting him to check for things that he does not yet realise are significant? Perhaps we need to explain that capital letters have to be used for proper nouns, or that that thing on the paper is not just a dirty mark but an apostrophe.

Or is it a matter of saying firmly: 'Hard luck. Get on with it'? Well, maybe, but even the most work-shy and careless need to take a break now and again. Avoid taking up the position of you-are-going-to-sit-there-until-you-find-it-and-it-is-your-fault-if-you-miss-football-practice. We do better to take in his work as far as he has got, tick the mistakes he has found and show pleasure that he has done so. Afterwards we can look through the mistakes that he has not found to see if there is any pattern in them. Is there anything particular that he does not seem to recognise? Or do we need to set a shorter, easy task for him in future so that even he will succeed? Or was it merely a Friday afternoon?

Spelling and dictation

Looking at spelling in general

In this chapter we consider how to help a child who has very poor spelling, having failed to respond to the school's usual methods of teaching spelling. We look, for example, not at spelling rules, but at how the child sets about analysing and memorising a spelling, and at how to improve his techniques. First, however, we consider what contributes to good spelling, the importance of accurate spelling, and how we may be able to improve our own spelling. We need to bear in mind that skills developed or neglected in one area of literacy may help or hinder progress in another. This certainly is so with spelling.

Good handwriting helps with spelling

Why do we need to learn a spelling? Not so that we can spell the word aloud but so that we can write it correctly while barely thinking about it. Fast, fluent handwriting can help us to acquire good spelling (through well-practised movements of joined-up writing which help us to remember letter sequence), as can well-formed, even writing (because we are able to match the shape of our writing with the shape of the word we are trying to spell). (See Chapter 7, Handwriting, and in particular: page 102, 'Very uneven handwriting'; page 108, 'Problems learning joined-up writing'; page 109, 'Uncovering poor spelling'. See also page 81, 'Shape', and page 137, 'Acquiring a physical habit'.)

Good copying skills help

By applying our minds when we copy a text, we are able to practise a spelling in context, analyse it as we go and link the sound and sight of it with the writing of it. (See Chapter 8 on Copying, and in particular page 115, 'Not analysing the word?' and 'Not saying the word?')

The spelling of each word has to be learnt separately. I may know how to spell fate, rate, gate, hate and Kate, but I cannot rely on the next word that sounds the same being spelt the same (wait, eight, straight, fête, great). I therefore need to find out the spelling of each new word if I am to be sure that I spell it correctly. (Is it frate, frait or freight?)

What implication does this have for the teaching of spelling? Well, teachers cannot possibly teach us the spelling of every word we are ever likely to want to write, so we are left to notice for ourselves how most words are spelt. Research has shown that we do not pick up much correct spelling just by the act of reading. What are we left with, then, apart from a dictionary? Copying, in my opinion. Every time we have occasion to copy a correct spelling and succeed in copying it correctly, we have had to look carefully at it and then practise it by writing it.

Using phonics helps

Knowing even a little about phonics makes spelling much easier, and means we are more likely to be able to make a reasonable guess at the spelling of a word or part of a word. There are many irregularly spelt words amongst the high-frequency words met in early reading, words such as 'who', 'one' and 'said'. A beginner reader who is confident with early phonics can use his knowledge to learn even those words by memorising them as they look phonically. For example, 'who' can be sounded as 'www-ho' to rhyme with 'go'. (See Appendix, 'Phonic generalisations' and 'Examples of phonic groups linked for spelling'.)

Good sensory learning habits help

We find it easier to master spellings, particularly difficult ones, if we link our different senses for maximum learning efficiency. (See Handwriting, pages 98-101, and Sight words, pages 71-72.)

Being a good reader does not necessarily help

As some people know only too well, it is possible to be an excellent reader but a terrible speller. This may have come about from a variety of causes, ranging from plain lack of adequate teaching, many changes of school, or speech or hearing problems, through to dyslexia or psychological factors. Most of these are beyond the scope of this book. However, we now consider a child who has apparently failed at an early stage to develop a sensory link in his mind between reading and spelling. Taking a simplistic example, suppose a beginner reader relies heavily on his visual memory without using the sound of words and parts of words to help him. Suppose that this same child learns to spell mainly by reciting words letter name by letter name (using his auditory sequential memory). Both learning methods are fine, but his learning would be strengthened if he linked the senses he uses for learning to read with those he uses for learning to spell.

Whether or not he makes a meaningful link may depend to a large extent, I suggest, on what he does when he copies words: that is, when he writes the word he has just read. If we are not up against emotional factors in his problem, it may be that we can encourage him to say the words or mouth them to himself. If he does this as he reads them and again as he writes them, he links by sound the word that he sees (reading) with the word that he writes down (spelling). (See bottom of page 44 and pages 115-116.) Note that here I am talking about an early learning technique. Continuing to say words aloud or in our heads long after we need to is not helpful (see pages 85-87).

Being good at spelling ourselves is not enough

If we are going to teach spelling, we need to be good at spelling. But that is only the start. Are we aware of our own methods of learning spellings? Are we aware – and this is crucial – that other good spellers may have different methods of learning from ourselves? (See page 130, 'Natural spellers and the rest of us'). What works for one person does not necessarily work for someone else. Therefore we need to offer children a wide variety of approaches – and offer it to all children, not just those with very obvious problems over spelling. We need to be ready and able to teach some children by fundamental methods met usually only in the first year or so in a good infant school.

Believing that spelling matters is essential

We let our pupils down if we do not convey the message, consciously and unconsciously, that we expect them to learn to spell correctly. Children need to learn the same rules of written communication in English as everyone else, as far as they are capable of doing so. It is not a matter of choice. If someone grows up indifferent to the rules and cannot be bothered to convey his or her meaning accurately, he or she runs the risk of being seen as slapdash, uneducated and unintelligent, and of not being understood.

Learning to spell accurately saves time and trouble in the long run. If I have to stop frequently to struggle to spell a word, or to decide on punctuation, I waste my time and break my train of thought. On the other hand I waste your time and risk exasperating you if I leave you to work out whether I mean peace, piece or peas, or if you have to reread and puzzle over my meaning because I have left out a crucial comma.

We need to sharpen a child's tools for written English and make sure he uses them well. If we improve a child's spelling, we improve his confidence, his written work and probably his reading. Even his handwriting may improve if he has deliberately made it illegible to cover up his spelling. In national exams he is less likely to lose marks for poor spelling, and he has better job prospects. He does not know this. We do. He needs our help.

Do we risk discouraging the child?

Do we risk discouraging a young child who is an extremely poor speller if we point out his spelling mistakes? Well, possibly, yes. We are not likely to improve his spelling ability,

Seb, aged 10, wrote an excellent piece about diamonds. A 'best' copy of this was exhibited in the school corridor. It contained 'diamonds' spelt 'dimonds' 17 times. Seb's teacher was adamantly against getting a child to write out spelling corrections even once, and yet allowed Seb to practise this incorrect spelling to excess.

however, if we do nothing about his mistakes. We need to concentrate first on the content of his written work, but to follow this up by analysing his misspellings in order to decide what help he needs next. We also do our best to provide him with a separate, correct version of one or more quality sentences derived from his work. We encourage him to read and copy these sentences, and, perhaps, to use the computer to produce an attractive printed version of them.

A child may make few mistakes but still be very weak in spelling. Harris, aged 10, was top of his year in maths but found spelling very difficult. The school was very keen on topic work, and spellings were not corrected. Harris set his own high standards and would write only words that he knew that he could spell. As a result, he often wrote only a bleak sentence or two. His class teacher spent much time teaching him spelling rules, to very little effect. Eventually, his confidence and his spelling improved significantly after several weeks of being allowed to dictate what he wanted to write. Copying his dictated work meant that he could see and practise the spellings he wanted.

What about spell-checkers?

Is a spell-checker the solution to spelling problems? Unfortunately, no. It is useful for picking up the occasional word we cannot spell or have mistyped, but to spell-check a document full of mistakes takes valuable time and is not completely effective either. The spell-checker may accept a correct spelling even though it is not the word we intended. We still have to decide between you, yew and ewe; faint and feint; bore, boar, boor or Boer. Similarly, the spell-checker will not alert us to 'Please repair stair winder', even though we intended the instruction to refer not to one of the steps on the turn of the stairs but to the window above them. And what if we have typed or spelt a word so badly that the spell-checker cannot find a likely word at all? Spelling is our responsibility.

Punctuation is our responsibility, too. No spell-check software can make the distinction between '"Hallo!" Uncle Jason said.' and '"Hallo, Uncle," Jason said.' (See page 65, 'Punctuation'.)

It is tough luck on some

Going back for a moment to Seb's spelling mistake (page 129), we need to consider the possibility that his teacher also could not spell 'diamond'. Many people who are teaching now grew up at a time when the teaching of spelling, formal grammar and multiplication tables was out of fashion. Some schools did not teach them. Some college lecturers told their students not to teach them. The consequences were dire. Eventually, when the current rethink about the basics has worked through primary schools, educational standards will rise. But many people have already missed out, including those now needing to teach spelling. So let us consider how we learn to spell, and what we can do to improve any weak areas we may have in our own spelling techniques.

Many ways of learning to spell

'Natural' spellers and the rest of us

Whether people develop into 'natural' spellers depends partly, I suspect, on what kind of teaching they receive.

A child with a strong visual memory is lucky. He is likely to find spelling relatively easy, no matter what approach is used, since he is seeing words all the time.

A child with a particularly strong auditory memory will thrive on a phonic approach to reading and spelling if given the chance. But what if his school uses only a sight-word, whole-sentence, whole-language or real-book approach to reading? And what if the only spelling help he is given amounts to little more than: 'Look at the word carefully'? Unless he develops phonic skills himself, he may well find learning to read and spell unnecessarily difficult.

Finally there is the child whose natural bent is to learn through the senses of touch and kinaesthesia (the awareness of the movement of the voluntary muscles and the position of the body). Children reinforce their learning through the act of writing and this is particularly so for this third type of child. He is one who is likely to try a spelling out by writing it with his finger on his knee or the table. Unfortunately for him, when schools got rid of dull old copy books, uninspiring traditional written exercises and the endless writing out of spelling corrections, they often rejected the very idea of learning through writing from a correct example – a case of throwing the baby out with the bath water. This child was thus left short of opportunities to learn spelling through his favoured senses.

Who knows how many more of us might have become 'natural' spellers if, in our early days at school, we had not been kept on a restricted literacy diet that did not happen to suit us? In spelling as in reading, people vary in the way they learn best, and we need to cater for those variations.

Are we using phonics to help?

Once we know the phonic probabilities, spellings begin to make more sense, especially if we say the words as we write them. For example, once we know the sound that *ir* usually indicates (as in 'bird'), the letter order of the word 'thirst' will make sense and we will not be tempted to spell it 'thrist'.

Are you arguing along the lines that you know *ir* but find that you still write 'thrist' instead of 'thirst'? If so, concentrate on saying the word as you write it, aloud or under your breath. Synchronise what you say with what you write. Do this even if the spelling is irregular as in 'beautiful': write ***beau*** while saying 'bew', then say and write ***ti***, then ***ful***. Say and write ***Wed-nes-day*** similarly. (See Phonics chapter; pages 143-144; Appendix, Phonic generalisations, pages 155-165; and suggestions for encouraging a new habit, pages 97-98.)

Keep applying your mind as you say and write a word simultaneously again and again until you have programmed your automatic pilot and you find you write the word correctly without thinking.

Copying carefully enough?

As a matter of interest, next time you copy a piece of writing, observe what you actually do. When you come to a spelling you have not yet learned, do you look carefully at it before you copy it? Do you notice its shape, length, and any familiar strings of letters? Do you check to see if the spelling matches the sound of the word or if there is a silent letter, or a vowel with an unexpected sound? If the spelling seems to be irregular do you think up a special way of remembering it? (For example, you might remember 'queue' not as ***qu*** + ***eue***, but as ***q*** + ***ue ue***. Then, while being aware it starts with ***q***, you might say it to yourself as 'kuh you-ee you-ee'.) Do you use the sound of each part of the word to guide you as you write it, and are you conscious as you copy that there has to be at least one vowel in every syllable? (***Y*** can be a vowel.)

All the above is good practice and well worth adopting if you have any trouble with spelling. Also, if you have analysed a long difficult word carefully and are about to copy it down, challenge yourself to write the whole of it from memory before looking back to check it. If you fail the first time, just keep trying. Even if it takes you several attempts it is better to do that than to copy only a bit of the word at a time. When you finally get it right, congratulate yourself warmly. Our memories thrive on praise. If you can go on to copy whole phrases or sentences at a time, so much the better because you will be practising spellings in context. Copying chunks out of a newspaper or magazine can be very helpful.

Checking carefully enough?

Do you usually give your finished work just a cursory glance, or not bother to check it at all? If so, now is the time to acquire a better habit and take control of your own work. The better we become at spotting our mistakes, the less likely we are to make them in the first place. (See pages 120-124, 'Self-checking what he has copied'.)

If your own spelling is not particularly good, ask yourself how you are feeling about all this spelling and self-checking. Are you bored? Resentful? Angry? Thinking it is all rather a waste of time? If you do happen to have feelings like that and have managed to get in touch with them, that can be very helpful. You will be able to recognise and understand those feelings in some of the children you teach. Check whether you have really decided to master spelling, or was it more a matter of thinking you ought to? Feeling helpless and pushed around by oughts, musts and shoulds is counter-productive. You can switch to 'I *choose* to', and then you are in charge.

Particularly difficult spellings

Probably all of us have words that give us trouble every time we have to write them. In the days of having to write sick notes for my children when yet another illness swept the schools, I had to consult my dictionary so often that it almost fell open by itself at the page for 'diarrhoea'. Eventually I mastered the wretched word by thinking of it as having 'two **r**s and a garden hoe'.

Here are some suggestions for catching your own particularly elusive spelling. Try learning it in a different way. Try whichever of the following ways you have not used before:

● say the whole word as you write it;

● spell it out as you write it;

● sound it out as you write it;

● concentrate on how it rhymes with another word;

- chant the letters in a distinctive rhythm, and clap or dance to the rhythm at the same time if it helps;

- type the word several times;

- write the word, hugely exaggerating the size and shape of the letters you find difficult to remember;

- write it with your finger on your knee or the palm of your other hand;

- write it with gaps between the syllables;

- visualise the difficult bit in a brilliant colour, and use a highlighter in the same way when writing the word;

- clap or stamp the word out letter by letter, or thump your fist into the palm of your other hand as you spell it;

- spell it with your eyes shut;

- recall it while you look upwards;

- write it twenty times, or even a hundred times, saying it and concentrating on it each time, and then recall it again in half an hour, two hours, the next morning, the next week;

- distinguish between two similar spellings by learning them in context (for example: 'over there' as opposed to 'their house'). When you copy a passage, remember to find out what the passage is all about first, and then copy down whole phrases at a time rather than single words. Knowing the context helps you associate a spelling with its meaning.

- link a difficult spelling with an easy one. For example:

    stationery: like writing a lett**er** on station**er**y
    stationary: like a c**ar** that is station**ar**y.

    It is best to work out your own links like this. What helps one person may not help another. But whatever link you make, visualise it in vivid colour and sound, and even make it a moving image if you can. Taking 'stationary' as an example, you might visualise a bright red car with a huge fluorescent *ar* on its door, and a rhythmic beat of music coming from inside.

Equipped for teaching

In this chapter so far we have looked at spelling in general. In my opinion, we need this broad yet detailed understanding if we are to tackle children's spelling problems effectively. We will now go on to look more specifically at how to tackle spelling problems on a broad front in the classroom, and then at individual problems still remaining.

Tackling spelling problems on a broad front

Can the children write their own names correctly?

Having looked in detail at our own spelling skills, we are in a better position to help children over their spelling problems. Let us start at the very beginning of spelling, and ask ourselves: can everyone in the class spell his own name? Can all the children write their names in reasonably correct handwriting for their age and ability? And if they know how to, do they do it?

If a child has not spelt his names correctly, talk to him about how they are spelt and suggest ways he could learn them (see page 143). Explain the difficult bit, for instance that the *ph* shows the same sound as a letter *f* does, or that there is a silent letter, or that his name is not spelt in a regular way so it is a matter of learning it letter by letter. Provide each child with a clearly written example of his name to keep and copy.

Then, if necessary, show each child how to write his name correctly. What part of handwriting does he find difficult? Does he need extra practice? See page 98 on forming a particular letter, page 102 for improving the relative size and position of his letters, page 105 for learning the difference between capital and small letters, pages 70-73 for help over reversing or inverting letters. As with spelling difficulties, provide the child with a clearly written example of his name to keep for reference.

A child may be forming letters incorrectly even though they look all right on paper. If you have any suspicions at all, check by watching how the child forms each letter as he writes his name for you with his finger on the table. Getting him to use his finger has advantages: it is quick and easy; without a pen and paper to remind him of what he ought to be doing, he is more likely to reveal what he usually does; and, if we need to teach him the correct formation, we are already in the basic sensory mode of touch and kinaesthesia.

Encourage all the children to take a pride in themselves and their names, and tell them that you expect them to write their names well at all times. Accept nothing less – not as a punishment but as a sign that you value them and that only the best is good enough for them. Show pleasure when they succeed and be sympathetic but firm if they have to rewrite their name on subsequent occasions. As they have the model to copy from, all they are required to do at present is to copy it correctly. If they still make mistakes, do they need more information on the model, such as a red dot where a letter starts or horizontal lines to show where letters are placed? Or is it that when not concentrating they have fallen back into old, incorrect ways? Rather than condemning this as 'mere carelessness', accept it as a real difficulty and explain how to get over it. (See page 97 for suggestions on correcting a bad habit.) Persevere. We can at least save children from the common street insult: 'He can't even write his own name properly.'

The vocabulary for spelling

The child needs to understand early on in spelling that no consonant 'says its name'. *D* is called 'dee' but 'Dund' is not enough to spell 'Dundee', and though *r* is called 'ar', it does not mean that 'rm' is enough to spell 'arm'. Every word and syllable have to have at least one vowel – and to understand this, the child needs to know that *y* can be either a consonant or a vowel. (Unless *y* starts a word it will act like the vowel *i*. See Appendix, pages 163-164.)

If we are to explain such things, the children need to understand the words we are using. While we talk about vowels and consonants to the class, an occasional child (and here I am referring to a native English speaker) may be trailing so far behind in language that he may be hazy about even such words as 'letter', 'line' and 'space'. We can help to a certain extent by getting into the habit of showing what we are talking about, pointing clearly on the board to the word or bit of word we mention, or moving our finger from side to side of a line, end to end of a sentence, or top to bottom of a paragraph. Note that we can teach the meaning of 'syllable' non-verbally. Try clapping out the 'lumps of sound' in words, as explained on page 58.

Grouping the phonic probabilities

For teaching reading, the customary advice is never to teach phonic groups together that have the same sound but different spellings. For example, never teach white, bite, kite at the same time as light, sight, fight. However, when it comes to teaching spelling, the opposite holds. A child who is having a go at an unknown spelling needs to be able to muster the likely choices in his mind, just as we do ourselves. Is it *ight* or *ite*? Is it *ir*, *ur* or *er*? Is it *f*, *ff* or *ph*? See Appendix, pages 167-169, 'Examples of phonic groups linked for spelling'.

Having a colour chart or pictures of animals on the wall is a useful way of reminding children of phonic groups, since so many colours and names of animals contain useful examples. (See lists on pages 166-167 of the Appendix.)

Acquiring a physical habit

No matter how we teach or learn spelling, the ultimate aim is to make the spelling of each word a physical habit of our hand so that we can write it with very little conscious thought.

If we want to walk across the room, most of us can do so without having to pay attention to the movements of our legs and the adjustment of our balance. If we want to cut an article out of the newspaper, most of us can use a pair of scissors to do so without hesitation. It was not so for any of us as infants.

We learnt very actively until we could do what we wanted to do, and subsequently have repeated those movements so often that they now scarcely intrude on our consciousness. We aim to spell words and common parts of words with the same habitual ease.

When we are dealing with children with spelling problems, underlining their misspelt word and writing it correctly for them is not enough in itself to motivate them to learn the spelling. Having to copy it at least once will mean that they have to pay some attention to the word, and writing it several times may help them to begin to see the pattern and feel the rhythm of writing it. (For some children it will be their preferred way of learning, using their senses of muscle movement and touch.) But practice on its own is dull. The child needs to see that it pays off by making written work easier, quicker and more accurate, and gains our attention and approval.

By the way, watch out for a child who decides to do his corrections downwards instead of across. For example, told to practise 'because' three times, he may write *b* three times in a descending line, then add an *e* to each of them, then *c* and so on. He has missed the point of the exercise (which was to practise the rhythmic sequence of the letters and/or the words in joined-up writing) and so is bored with what appears to be a meaningless task. Explain and convince him that it is not a punishment but a way of helping him learn.

If the child's work is peppered with misspellings (and also, probably, mistakes in punctuation and in the use of capital letters), the last thing he needs is to have to write out spelling corrections three times. He is not at that stage. Respond to the content of his writing and then give him a chance to copy part or all of his work accurately. He may need to work from a fair copy, handwritten or typed.

Rote learning

Do not underestimate the usefulness of rote learning. Some children benefit greatly from spelling out words alphabetically in a rhythmic chant with the rest of the class.

('B-i-r-t-h-d-a-y spells birthday. P-a-r-t-y spells party.') Rote learning went out of fashion but the fact remains that some children are not only helped by it but clearly enjoy it. Perhaps some also find it a relief and a comfort to do something so straightforward, predictable and safe.

Use the words on the board or on cards that you hold up. Read out the word first (in case someone cannot read it), then point to each letter in turn as the class says it, and finish by everyone saying what the word is. Pointing to the letters may not be necessary for older children but can be helpful to a younger child who is not yet sure of the names of letters – helpful, that is, as long as he looks at each letter as he says it.

Next the children chant the spellings without looking at them. This is harder. Repeating the same spelling several times and practising it again a few hours, days and weeks later digs it deeper into our memory.

The Great Mistake Hunt

We can set up an on-going Mistake Hunt. Anyone who can prove with the use of a dictionary that we have made a spelling mistake earns a reward or special recognition of some sort. The mistakes can be deliberate or accidental. If your spelling is shaky, setting up a mistake hunt like this is very motivating and beneficial! The children usually love it, and groups of them will happily (and usefully) pore over dictionaries that might otherwise lie neglected.

Using spelling tests effectively

Getting one's feet on the ground

Over the page you will see the story of Alistair and the weekly spelling tests set by his school. But that episode happened long ago. Alistair's teacher has long since retired, Alistair has long since left school, and there have been many changes in that school and in schools in general. So is there any point in bringing up the story? Oh, yes. In 1996, some twenty years later, in a primary school in a different part of the country, Alistair's young cousin, Roddy, was performing as badly in his

Alistair, aged 10, was judged by his junior school head to be one of the brightest in his year. Each week his class had spellings to copy down and take home to learn over the weekend, ready for a test. Alistair copied them down carelessly and made no attempt to learn them. He scored badly each week in the test, but with impunity. He was not asked to explain his poor performance and did not have to correct his work. Nothing happened except another list, another test, the next week, for over two terms.

What did he learn from this weekly activity? Absolutely nothing (except that spelling tests did not matter). Finally, in the summer term, his parents came across one of his copied lists by chance, stared in disbelief at words so misspelt that many were unidentifiable, and began to ask questions.

weekly spelling tests. Nearly eight years old and of well above average intelligence, he too suffered no recrimination. No comments were made about his poor performance, no corrections demanded. Just another test the next week. Luckily for him he experienced only one term of such a futile activity before his parents, in their turn, looked aghast at a list of incorrect and unidentifiable spellings. They resorted to paying for private lessons to ensure that their son learnt to work to a better standard, and eventually they switched him to another primary school.

Weekly spelling tests do not have to be a deplorable waste of time, nor just a formality to keep parents and school governors happy. Indeed, we can use the weekly tests to teach spelling and related skills profitably. How? You may well ask that if your own experience of school spelling tests was unluckily anything like that of Alistair and Roddy.

Both teachers involved were clearly floundering and, unless we are to believe in a quite extraordinary coincidence, others may well be, too. What detailed, specific help might such teachers need if they are to make weekly spelling tests more effective? I offer the following as a pointer towards the sort of broad-based approach to the tests that I believe would be helpful. It is not intended as a model to be slavishly followed. Children, schools, our own experience, abilities and inclinations, all vary, and so do the ways we teach. I offer only a rough sketch of a general rescue plan which would have to be adapted to fit circumstances. Someone in danger of drowning needs to be brought to dry land. Experienced rescuers could, doubtless, carry out the rescue more skilfully, and might pick a better part of the beach or the coast, but they are not here. By following the spirit of my plan, the teacher in difficulty at least has a chance to get his or her feet on the ground, and decide where to go from there. Of course they may go straight back into the water and carry on drowning, which is their choice but very unfair on the children they teach.

I suggest that you may find the following rescue plan relevant even if you run your spelling tests well and in a very different way or have no intention of using such tests at all.

A plan for making the most of weekly tests

Here is a summary of steps I suggest for running weekly spelling tests, followed by a detailed explanation of each step. (But before you start, have you ensured that everyone in the class can write or copy his or her name correctly and in reasonably good handwriting – and do you expect them to do so? If there is any doubt about this, please turn to page 135 as a matter of priority.)

1. Choose up to five words.

2. Talk about each word, write it on the board, and show how you would set about learning it.

3. Get the children to copy the words. Make sure that they do

so correctly and in good handwriting. If any of them do not, help them with their difficulty, and get them to copy the whole list correctly this time on a new sheet of paper.

4. Tell the children to take the spellings away and learn them thoroughly. Give the children an opportunity to practise them in class also.

5. Test the children a few days later.

6. Deal with whatever the test results reveal.

Step 1. Choose the words

Why pick only five spellings or fewer? Because we are aiming for quality of learning rather than quantity at the moment. And what five do you pick? Classes vary so much that only you can decide that. You cannot go far wrong if you use Schonell's spelling list or a similar one. Start at an easy level because we want everyone to feel confident that they can spell some words and that they can get things right and get ticks. (That is a rare and exhilarating feeling for some children in some classes.)

Once you have gained confidence and know your children's spelling capability well, you might follow the practice of a very experienced colleague of mine. She uses Schonell's list, but also chooses five words or more of her own on occasions, to fit what she is particularly wanting to teach. She starts with a very simple phonic spelling, then follows perhaps with a word with a double letter (two *l*s, for example); then a word in which the child has to remember something phonically special such as *ow* in the middle or a marker *e*; then a long word that breaks up into easy, phonically regular syllables; and finally a tricky word that is not spelt as it sounds (e.g. come, yacht, bury). If we point out: 'This last one is a very tricky one', we imply that the children are going to be very clever to spell it, with the result that if they succeed they are going to feel very pleased with themselves and if they fail they will not feel crushed. Spelling taught by an inspired teacher can be satisfying and fun.

Step 2. Talk about the words and how they are spelt

Explain to the class that you are going to talk about how certain words are spelt. Tell them that they will have a spelling test on these words at another time, but that at the moment you want everyone just to listen and watch.

> *N.B. Face the class, move your lips clearly and articulate well as you say each spelling. Make sure the children are looking at your mouth as you do so.*

Say the first word. Make sure that everyone knows which word you are talking about by using it in context. For example, 'Rain. Like: There are black clouds and it looks as if it is going to rain.'

Write the word on the board, saying it complete syllable by complete syllable. For example, 'rain' or 'be-cause' or 'an-i-mal'. End up by saying the whole word normally again.

Now talk about how this particular word is spelt and how you would learn it. For example:

rain   Link it with 'train' and 'again', point out the *ai*, and sound it out: 'r-ai-n'. Then write it again on the board, showing how you are saying the word to synchronise with what you are writing. So, with this one-syllable word, you prolong it so that it starts and finishes as your writing does: 'rrrainnn'. End by saying the word normally.

because   Warn the children that this is one of the words that is not spelt exactly as it sounds, so they will have to find their own way of remembering it. Suggest they could say it letter name by letter name, over and over again. They could then write it several times, saying the whole word as they do so. Or they could write it while saying it to rhyme with 'pause' (be-cause). Emphasise that the important thing is to learn it. Now write it again on the board, showing how you synchronise each syllable with the writing of it, prolonging it as above. Write it twice, showing the alternative ways of

143

thinking about it: 'beee-cozzz', 'beee-cauzzz'. End by saying the word normally.

animal   Pronounce the word particularly clearly, and emphasise the short *i* sound in the middle, in case the children are hearing it as 'er' or 'a'. The indeterminate vowel sound of the last syllable could be spelt in other ways ('el' as in parcel, 'le' as in little, and so on), so suggest they say 'mal' very clearly to rhyme with 'pal' – 'my pal the animal'. Then write it on the board again, pointing out that you prolong each syllable as you say it to synchronise with each syllable as you write it: 'annn-i-mmmalll'. End by saying the word normally.

It is important to finish by saying the whole word again normally. It is the whole word that the children are having to remember, not just its bits.

Get them to practise, writing with their finger on the desk or table or their knee or the palm of their other hand, and saying the word as you have said it. Check that they are doing it properly.

Step 3. Copying the spellings

Give each child a separate piece of paper. Tell them to put their names and the date at the top and then to copy the list of words carefully. Explain that writing the words in good handwriting will help them to remember them. (Make sure that the date is somewhere in full view and clearly written in large enough writing.)

Take in the copied lists and check both spelling and handwriting very thoroughly. This is an opportunity to set high standards for a small limited task. Your aim is for every child to have a correct and well-written list of the spellings that he has to learn. Of course you could hand out a duplicated list, but it would be a pity to forego this small handwriting and copying lesson if standards in the class are dire and the children need help of this kind as a matter of top priority.

Check the child's name. Expect it to be correctly spelt and written (see page 135). Then check the spelling of the date and the five words, and then how well they have been written. What do you find?

- A few children making a few mistakes? Point out to each child what he has got wrong and write a clear model for him to copy.

- A single child with all sorts of copying and handwriting errors? For the moment, write out his name, the date and the five words for him, provided that he can read them. That ensures he has a correct list to take home. Perhaps, in addition, write one or all of the words (large and clear) on another sheet of paper for him to copy underneath. Assess the situation after you discover how well he copies this, and how well he does later in the spelling test.

- Half the class writing very badly? This is something you will need to tackle energetically and urgently, but not at this minute. (See the Handwriting chapter and particularly pages 109-110.) For now, pick one word on each paper, and write it correctly to be copied.

Hold on to the correct lists, and get all the others corrected properly and handed back for you to check again. What if the child has written his or her name incorrectly? Perhaps try something along these lines: 'I am sad when I see your name misspelt/written illegibly. It needs to be corrected.' Treat the matter quietly and firmly. Remember to comment positively when he does it correctly unprompted, and to keep commenting positively from time to time in future to show him that you notice that he is keeping up the improvement.

Step 4. Learning the spellings

Once all corrections have been done, give all the children their lists to take home and learn ready for a test. For a variety of reasons some children will get no help at home. You may be aware of some of these children, but unknown others may be ploughing lonely furrows. So provide some short practice sessions in class, and encourage children also to practise with a friend.

Step 5. The test itself

Give out pieces of paper. The children put their names and the date on them as usual.

Read out the spellings one by one in a different order from the one they copied. Tell the children to write them in a list. 'I shall say every word twice. If you miss it when I say it the first time, listen very carefully and wait for me to say it again. Number one: because.' (Repeat the word after three or five seconds.) 'Number two: Wednesday' and so on. If the spelling depends on the meaning, put the word in context. For example, with 'stare' as opposed to 'stair', you might say: 'Number three: stare. Like "Don't stare at him."' Remember to face the class, speak clearly and move your lips.

Tell the children to check their work for any mistakes. Running their finger or pen along each word will help to direct their eyes and their minds. Then collect in the papers.

Step 6. Deal with whatever the results reveal

Check through all the papers, highlighting any mistakes in spelling. There should be few, if any, after all those preliminaries. Get the children to write out their corrections at least three times, perhaps ten times depending on the child and the mistake. In subsequent weeks keep working at the standard of copying and of handwriting for these spelling tests. Until the standard improves considerably you are going to have a lot of spelling and handwriting corrections to deal with, so I suggest that you continue to set only a small number of spellings each week, though you may want to alter the level of difficulty.

If a number of children have made spelling mistakes, what might be the cause? Have you chosen spellings that are too difficult? Or do you need to rethink what you explain and demonstrate in Step 2? Were you earnestly teaching abstract spelling rules when all you needed to do at this stage was to point out a silent letter or a doubled one, or to teach that **au** has the same sound as in 'August' and 'astronaut'? Have a look at the type of mistakes made. Can they tell you anything about what you need to point out next time? For example, if several people have reversed letters, they are probably not matching what they are saying with what they are writing, or not bothering to say the word at all. Finally, consider the possibility that there were a lot of mistakes in the test because you have not yet convinced the class that everyone now has to work to a high standard. Keep reminding yourself that you are battling *for* the children and their educational future.

Make no big issue of mistakes, but quietly and firmly get corrections done properly. You are not going to give anyone the pleasure of winding you up by not working well. Instead, you aim to reward them with a warm smile or comment when they eventually produce work to your standard, or are clearly trying at last to do so.

Do you remember to comment warmly in the same way on the good work of children who always produce good work? It can seem unfair to them if we take their high standard for granted and comment only when it slips slightly.

In general, show the children their progress and how pleased you are that they are making it. A 'Wow!' can go a long way – provided you are genuinely appreciating the child's success. 'That was a very tricky spelling, and you got it right' can send a low-achiever home glowing with accomplishment.

The child whose spelling is still not improving

What have we missed?

Now we consider the child with particular difficulties over spelling and who continues to spell badly despite all our efforts and our broad-based approach to spelling (as considered on pages 135-139). This does not mean that we are about to plunge into a study of dyslexia. That is beyond the scope of this book. But not all dreadful spellers are dyslexic – as we shall see with Melanie (page 151) – and anyway the fact that a child has been professionally diagnosed as dyslexic is no reason for us to opt out of trying to help him in the classroom.

Ask the child about his difficulty

Have we asked the very poor speller what he finds difficult about spelling? His answer may be enlightening. (One child's reply revealed an eyesight problem.)

Can he tell us what is going on in his mind as he tries to spell a word? He may not understand what exactly we are wanting to know. Explain that it would be a great help to us to know how he goes about spelling a word. Does he say the letter names in his head? Or does he use phonics? Or does he say the word as a whole? Does he try to remember another word like it? Does he just remember the word as an image with no sound? Or does he do something else? Explain that there are no right or wrong answers. As he may never have thought about what exactly he was doing before, he may need to try spelling several words before he can tell us. Thank him sincerely for his help.

What has his answer revealed, and what can we do to help? (See Sight words chapter, pages 113-116 of Copying, and the list of suggestions on pages 133-135 of this chapter.)

Has the child seen what spelling is all about?

Has the child realised that there is a link between the sound and the spelling of most words?

Owain, aged 10, was a good reader for his age but found spelling difficult. I was asked if I would include him in a small mixed-age junior group that I had started taking once a week for spelling problems. He joined the group on the day that, by luck, I was demonstrating how to say a word while writing it. 'Oh, I get it!' he exclaimed in excitement after about ten minutes. 'It connects!' Judging from the rapid improvement he made in the rest of that lesson, something

Malcolm, a retired head teacher, was helping a middle-aged man with severe spelling problems. Malcolm pointed out that the man would be able to spell a word like dog if he sounded it out: d-o-g.

The man groaned, 'Is that what you do? Why didn't anyone tell me?'

certainly had connected. He explained afterwards that he knew how to sound out words when reading but that he had never realised before that he could reverse the process and use the sounds of English to help work out spellings. We mutually agreed that there was no need for him to continue in the group. He stopped me in the corridor a few weeks later to thank me again and tell me how much easier he found spelling now.

What can we learn from misspellings?

A spelling is not right until it is completely right. There is no such thing as a 60 per cent pass mark for a spelling. It is either totally correct or we have not yet learnt it.

This is not to reject out of hand every misspelling. On the contrary, if we can find the time, there is much to be gained from analysing which spelling-attack skills were used, and which are still to be taught – provided we make a note of it. We also help and encourage the child by acknowledging what he has done right. The child becomes more consciously aware of what strategies he uses, and knows that we understand his efforts. We then go on to suggest what else he needs to know or do to spell that particular word. 'I see you tried to sound it out. Well done.' Then point out that the word has two *t*s, or commiserate with him because it is an irregular spelling, or teach him how to pronounce the word correctly if that was what let him down, and so on.

Take the example of a child who has written *l* perhaps instead of *d* or *b*. It looks as if he has relied on remembering the look of the word and has not used the sound of it. If this is so, he has either not learnt phonics at all, even though we may be under the impression that we had taught him adequately (see pages 43-45 and 47, and also page 13 for the definition of the verb 'to teach'), or he is not linking what phonics he knows with what he writes (see pages 57-58 and 115-116). We need to spring into action. Explain that trying to remember what the word looks like is fine as far as it goes, but that he needs also to use the sound of the word to help him. Demonstrate how to say the word, syllable by long-drawn-out syllable, as you write it, and get him to copy you. Then make sure you keep an eye on the situation.

Does the child need to learn spellings in context?

If a child has great difficulty learning spellings, does he invariably try to learn single words on their own or in a list? He may find it easier to remember a spelling when he has seen it in context, copied it in context, and can link it to a familiar phrase or sentence. (See pages 114-115.) Learning in context is not just for trying to distinguish between the spelling of similar-sounding words like pair, pear and pare, but builds up our general awareness of spelling.

Once, when giving a talk on spelling, I asked a group of teachers to copy something from the board. I had deliberately chosen a paragraph from a scientific article containing several unfamiliar words. Stopping the group when they had barely started, I asked who had glanced through the passage first to see what it was about. Only two had not done this, and they were the only two who confessed they were poor spellers. Coincidence?

Looking is not enough

Is the child not looking carefully enough at the spelling of a word? We need to perceive, to be able to look at the word meaningfully, see its structure, be aware of its context, link it with the way other words and parts of words are spelt. A 'careless' speller may never have looked carefully enough. Check his copying skills (see page 113 onwards) and make sure that he writes out any corrections several times and in his best handwriting. This will help him learn that particular word and may encourage him to focus his mind more carefully on words in future.

Melanie, nearly nine years old, had great difficulty over spelling. When asked to look carefully at a word of four or five letters and then copy it down from memory she often made curious mistakes. I then tried her on Kim's Game. In the game the players look at a number of objects for a short time before the objects are covered up or removed. The players have to try to recall them all. The game is called after Rudyard Kipling's book, *Kim*, in which the young boy, Kim, is being groomed as a British agent in India. After being shown some precious stones for a short time, he has to try to describe them from memory. Melanie played this game several times with other children and she was the only one who could not remember all five ordinary objects such as a torch battery or a comb.

I remonstrated, 'Melanie, I told you to look carefully.'

'Oh, I did, Miss. Really I did!' There were tears in her eyes.

I was baffled. Long seconds must have passed before a wild idea occurred to me. 'Melanie, when you looked at the things, did you do anything else? Did you name them? Did you say to yourself: a comb, a battery, a ribbon, and so on?'

Melanie sounded mystified at such a suggestion. 'No, Miss, I just looked.'

Much relieved that I had got to the bottom of the problem, I explained that when I played the game I told myself what the things were. If I did not know the name of something I would try to describe it in some way: 'The little thing you bang into wood' or 'A soft white thing'. Did Melanie think she could try doing that? Yes, Melanie did think so, and went on to list all the new objects when we played the game again. Later I got her to name letters and words in the same way, and her spelling began to improve.

Chapter 9

Have we labelled the child?

Is the child merely living down to our expectations of him? We need to become aware of how we, the child and the parents refer to the child's spelling. 'He's a dreadful speller.' 'He's just like his Dad, hopeless at spelling.' 'I can't spell.' These are not helpful statements.

We need to try to counter such labelling. Changing our way of talking can help a lot. If we stop thinking about him as 'a dreadful speller' and think of him instead as someone who 'finds spelling very difficult at the moment', we introduce hope for change and success. The statement 'He can't spell' or 'I can't spell' needs to be challenged. If there is even one word that he can spell (cat? dog? his name? his favourite football team?), then he can spell – not a lot, but he has made a start. He has made a start to spelling even if he is getting just the first letter or two right.

If we change our own way of thinking and talking about the child and his spelling and raise our expectations of him, it can have very positive results. He can begin to see himself differently and gain confidence, and maybe the parents will begin to see him differently too. It is not easy to take off a label. Occasionally we may come across a family who seem determined to keep it on.

When relationships are a problem

Are we getting nowhere with a child? He does not appear to be lacking in ability but is making no progress in spelling? Try him on his own on a computer, with a spelling game or an educational adventure game of the sort that will only accept correctly spelt instructions ('Dig hole', 'Walk to castle'). This is not a matter of indulging the child. It is just that he may be one who finds relationships with all other people difficult. In general and not just for spelling, he may find it easier to learn when interacting only with a piece of software. Also try using his personal dictation. Type it and get him to copy it accurately (see pages 20-22). Or type his usual work both accurately and as spelt, for 'Spot the Difference'.

Dictation

Why dictation?

Dictation helps children develop their skill of translating what they hear into what they write. The mistakes they make help us to identify and deal with their mispronunciations and misunderstandings. 'Wunser poner time' and 'Aunt they here?' may come to light, as well as 'so the man carry Don down the road'. By making up a passage of prose for dictation that includes words learnt for previous weekly spelling tests, we can use dictation to revise spellings. Writing those spellings in context like this can help some children to bridge the gap between what they get right in a spelling test and what they use in their own writing. We can also use dictation to practise punctuation.

The knack of writing to dictation

Children accustomed to written spelling tests have already acquired some of the skills needed to take down dictation successfully. They have learned that they need to listen or they will miss the next word. They will have discovered that we do not wait for them to catch up.

Give the children a chance to practise. Start with a short, easy passage. Face the class and speak clearly. Dictate in short phrases rather than in single – words – like – this. Repeat each phrase once. At the end read the whole passage through again slowly, without pausing. Make sure each child takes this opportunity to check his work, preferably running his finger or pen along the line as he hears the words.

Expect wails of 'Wait! Wait!', as they lag behind, and other wails of 'What did you say?' when they were not listening. Teach them that it is better to leave gaps and unfinished words than to be left behind and miss the next words. They will have a chance to fill in the gaps when you read right through at the end.

Expect an occasional child to continue to struggle with a difficult or unknown spelling regardless of being left behind.

In his experience, half-finished words and gaps would get him into trouble. You are trying to get him to work in an entirely new way for dictation and he may need quite a bit of reassurance before he does so.

What do you do about correcting this practice work? I recommend writing the original text on the board and going through it with the children. Let them correct their own work and learn from their mistakes. Make it clear that you want them to get used to taking dictation, and that you do not mind about mistakes yet because it is just a practice. Take in their corrected work afterwards to see how they are doing.

When the children have got the idea of dictation you can correct their work properly and give marks for it. What you do about corrections depends on the mistakes. Talking about the error may be sufficient, but sometimes the child will need to practise a spelling or whole phrase several times or learn by copying out the whole passage correctly.

You can give the dictation unseen or you can prepare the children for it in the same way as for the weekly spelling tests (see page 141). Write the dictation on the board and read it aloud, making sure that everyone understands it and knows what the words mean. Then go through it, pointing out difficult spellings, abbreviations, punctuation, etc. Get the children to copy it correctly, tell them to learn how to write it, and then test them on it.

Phonic generalisations

This list is not meant to be exhaustive. Nor should it be taken to imply that all the phonic groups should be taught, nor that they should be taught in the order they are listed.

The sounds of individual letters

a   as in *apple, ant.*

b   as in *baby, bottle.*

c   as in *cup, camel.*
(Not *c* before *e*, *i* and *y*, which is soft as in *centre, city, cycle*. This is usually taught later. See page 163, **soft c**.)

d   as in *dog, dandelion.*

e   as in *elephant, egg.*

f   as in *fish, fence.*

g   as in *gate, girl.*
(*g* may be soft before *e*, *i* or *y* as in *gentle, giant, gypsy*. This is usually taught later. See page 163, **soft g**.)

h   as in *horse, hat.*

i   as in *igloo, iguana.*

j   as in *jug, jam.*

k   as in *king, kangaroo.*

l   as in *lion, ladybird.*

m   as in *mirror, mouse.*

n   as in *nut, nest.*

o   as in *orange, ostrich.*

p   as in *pig, panda.*

qu   as in *queen, quick.*

r   as in *rabbit, red.*

s   as in *sandal, sock.*

t   as in *tiger, table.*

u   as in *umbrella, upstairs.*

v   as in *violin, vegetables.*

w   as in *window, wasp.*

x   as in *six, fox.* This is the sound of ***x*** anywhere in a word except at the beginning. The sound of ***x*** at the beginning of a word is 'zzz', but it occurs so rarely that the only examples most of us will meet are *xylophone*, *Xerxes* and *xerox*. Compilers of alphabet books may resort to *X-ray* or *Xmas*. Some avoid illustrating ***x*** at all.

y   as in *yellow, yacht.* This is the sound of ***y*** only when it occurs at the beginning of a word. Anywhere else in a word ***y*** acts like ***i***. See pages 163-164, ***y as a vowel***.

z   as in *zebra, zip.*

Saying the sounds of consonants

How we say the sounds of the consonants in isolation is very important. Saying them with a heavy 'uh' or 'er' sound at the end makes it harder to work out a word. If a child tries to read the word 'but', and says *buh-u-tuh* (or *ber-u-ter*) very heavily, he has to struggle to make sense of it and may well guess 'butter'. So we make the sounds of the following letters very light and crisp, keeping the inevitable vowel sound at the end as short and unobtrusive as possible: *b*, *c*, *d*, *g*, *k*, *p*, *t*.

However, for the same reason, some consonants are better prolonged. *Mmm-a-nnn* may lead to 'man'. *Muh-a-nuh* (or *mer-a-ner*) is more likely to lead to 'manner' – if not to frustration. So we prolong the following:

f   *fff* (i.e. instead of 'fuh' or 'fer'). Prolong the beginning of *finger* or *foot*.

h   A voiceless *h* – like breathing on glasses before cleaning them. Not like a voiced 'huh' of disbelief or disapproval. Prolong the beginning of *hair* or *hat*.

j   Prolong the beginning of *jug* or *jacket*.

l   Like the end of an exhortation to 'Pull-l-l!' Prolong the beginning of *leg* or *lip*.

m   *mmm*. The sound of agreement. Prolong the beginning of *mouth* or *man*.

n   *nnn*. Prolong the beginning of *nose* or *neck*.

qu   *kwww*. Prolong the beginning of *queen* or *question*.

r   *rrr*. Prolong the beginning of *rabbit* or *robin*.

s   *sss* (hiss). Prolong the beginning of *sock* or *sausage*.

v   *vvv* (this makes one's lips tingle). Prolong the beginning of *vase* or *volcano*.

w   *www*. Prolong the beginning of *wood* or *Wednesday*.

x   *ksss*, like the end of *fox* or *six*. The sound of *x* at the beginning of a word is 'zzz', but occurs so rarely that words like *xylophone, Xerxes* and *xerox* are better learnt as sight words.

z *zzz*. Prolong the beginning of *zoo, zebra* or *zip*.

sh, ch
and th When making the sound of these consonant digraphs, avoid saying them as 'shuh', 'chuh' and 'thuh' (or 'sher', 'cher' and 'ther'), but prolong them, e.g. ***sh*** as in 'Shhh! Be quiet!'

sh as in *shoe, shop, shark, shell, sheep, shut*.

ch as in *cheese, chips, chimpanzee* or the end of *rich* or *much*.

th (1) voiceless, as in *thumb, thistle, thanks* or the end of *bath* or *teeth*.
(2) voiced, as in *the, these, those* or the end of *bathe* or *smooth*.
N.B. ***th*** is not always taught as two sounds. Often only the voiceless sound is taught, leaving the very common words with a voiced ***th*** to be partly guessed, partly learnt as sight words, since they are so common. E.g. *the, they, them, their, these, those, this, that, then, than, other, another, mother, father, brother, weather, whether, either*.

Consonant clusters

Initial consonant clusters: ***bl, br, cl, cr, dr, dw, fl, fr, gl, gr, pl, pr, sk, sl, sm, sn, sp, st, sw, tr, tw, scr, spl, spr, squ, str*** and ***sc*** (except for words beginning ***sce, sci***, for which see ***soft c***, page 163). Also ***shr, thr***.

End clusters: ***ck, st, ct, ft, ld, lk, lf, lp, lt, mp, nd, nk, nt, pt, sk, sp, xt*** and ***nch, tch, lth***.

(See Phonics chapter, pages 38-39 and page 54.)

More phonic generalisations

ng a nasal sound as follows:

ing as in *thing, sing, string, king, ring, wing, bring, finger,* and all the words with an added *-ing* such as *walking, running, seeing, singing, ringing.*

ang as in *bang, rang, sang,* and words like *angle, tangle* and *anger.*

ong as in *long, song, strong, Hong Kong, belong, wrong* and words like *longer, stronger.* (Exception: *tongue.*)

ung as in *lung, sung, stung, sprung, flung, rung.* (This is only a small group.)

eng in *length, strength.* (These two could be learnt as sight words.)

oo **long oo** as in *zoo, kangaroo, shampoo, food, mood, pool, cool, shoot, boot, root, loop, loose, moon, soon, afternoon, tooth.*

short oo as in *book, took, look, cook, hook, foot, good, wood, hood, wool.*

Sometimes only the long sound of **oo** is taught, from which words with the short sound may be guessed. (*Room* and *broom* may be pronounced either way.)
(Common exceptions: *blood, flood.*)

ee as in *see, chimpanzee, Dundee, eel, feel, peel, seem, indeed, feed, seed, weed, greedy, seek, leek, feet, keep, deep, weep, peep, meet, teeth.*

final e (vowel-consonant-e) This silent final *e* is also known as marker *e*, magic *e* and lengthening *e*. Its presence can

indicate that the preceding vowel is 'long'.
It is sometimes taught as: 'The *e* makes the
vowel say its name.' The following paired
words illustrate this: *tap, tape; mad, made;
pal, pale; them, theme; pet, Pete; pip, pipe;
fin, fine; kit, kite; rod, rode; hop, hope;
us, use; tub, tube.*

a-e as in *gate, cake, whale.*
(Common exceptions: *have,* and *ate* when
this is pronounced to rhyme with *bet.*)

e-e as in *Christmas Eve, these, athlete, stampede,*
and when *r* is the middle letter, as in: *here,
sphere, mere, sincere.*
(Common exceptions: *there, where, were.*)
(**e-e** does not occur frequently, and few
examples occur in early reading.)

i-e as in *white, kite, bride, alive, drive.*
(Common exceptions: *give,* and *live* when
it rhymes with *give.* Also nearly all multi-
syllable words ending in *-ive* and *-ice.*)

o-e as in *nose, bone, home.*
(Common exceptions: *one, done, gone, some,
come, become, love, dove, shove, glove, above.*)

u-e as in *tune, use, refuse.* Also when the *u* is
pronounced 'oo' as in *June, rude, prune.*

ea **long ea** as in *sea, tea, eat, seat, real, mean,
each.* Also in *lead* (*dog's lead*) and *read* ('*Read
this*').

short ea as in *bread, deaf, head, weather, feather,
measure, instead.* Also in *lead (heavy as lead),*
and *read* ('*Have you read this?*')
(Common exception: *great.*)

final le **short vowel-2 consonants-le** as in *bottle, little, saddle, muddle, apple, puddle, handle, bundle, crumple.*

long vowel-consonant-le as in *table, stable, title, noble, able, scruple.*
(Exceptions: when *-able, -ible* are suffixes, as in *knowledgeable, moveable, impossible.*)

ai as in *rain, train, snail, tail, paid.*
(Common exception: *said.*)

air as in *air, chair, pair, stairs, hair, repair.*

ay as in *day, play, say, May, way, away.*
(Exceptions: *says, quay.*)

oa as in *road, soap, coat, goal, toast, toad.*
(Exceptions: *broad, abroad, oasis.*)

ow (1) as in *cow, now, how, down, town, owl, brown, vowel.* Also in *row* (argument), *sow* (pig), *bow* (bow down).
(2) as in *snow, grow, low, show, own, below, narrow, shadow.* Also in *row* (boat), *sow* (seeds), *bow* (tie).

ou as in *out, about, house, round, pound, found, loud.*
(Various exceptions include *could, would, should, country, trouble* and *wound* [injury].)

aw as in *saw, draw, law, awful, awkward, dawn, yawn, trawler.*

au as in *Paul, August, daughter, author, automatic, astronaut, haunt.*
(Exceptions include *aunt, because, laugh,* and *fault* if pronounced to rhyme with *bolt.*)

oi as in *oil, toilet, coin, noise, avoid, join, voice, appointment, disappointed.*
(Exceptions: *tortoise, coincide, heroic, stoic.*)

Appendix

oy as in *boy, toy, enjoy, annoy, employ, Roy, royal, oyster*. (This is only a small group.)

ar as in *car, star, far, park, dark, arm, farm, hard, art, part, carpet*.
(Exceptions: words with *war* as in *war, warm, warn, wart, warp, swarm*. See **wa**, **wo**, page 164.)

are as in *care, rare, glare, bare, spare, fare, stare*.
(Exception: *are*.)

ir as in *girl, birthday, first, thirsty, fir, dirty, shirt*.

ire as in *fire, spire, tired, umpire, desire, enquire, shire*.
(Exception: county names such as *Oxfordshire, Yorkshire*.)

ight as in *fight, right, night, knight, might, bright, tight, frightened, height*.
(Exceptions: *eight, weight, freight*.)

ur as in *turn, burn, hurt, church, fur, surname, burst, urgent, surgery*.
(Exceptions: *bury, jury, fury, burrow, furrow*.)

ure as in *cure, pure, temperature, nature, mixture, picture, future, capture, figure, furniture, adventure*. (Note that the vowel sound varies between **long u**, **oo**, and an indeterminate sound as in *figure*.)

ph as in *Philip, photograph, phone, pheasant, phonics, philosopher, sphere, atmosphere*.
(Exception: *shepherd*.)

wh as in *white, wheel*.
(Exceptions: *who, whom, whose;* and *whole, wholly, whooper swan, whore*.)

ew as in *new, few, Matthew*, and in *grew, flew, Andrew*. (Note the pronunciation varies between **long u** and **oo**.)

dge as in *edge, bridge, badger, hedge, hedgehog, judge, budget.*

soft c When followed by *e, i* or *y, c* becomes soft ('sss') as in:

> **ce** as in *centre, certain, cease,* and all words ending in -*ce* such as *ice, rice, price, prince, race, face, space.*

> **ci** as in *city, cinema, science, circle, circus, scissors.* (But see **-ci + vowel**, page 165.)

> **cy** as in *cycle, cyclamen, icy, juicy, Lucy, Tracy, emergency.*

soft g When followed by *e, i* or *y, g* is sometimes soft like *j* as in the following examples:

> **ge** as in *gentle, generally, gerbil, germ, genius, geography, George, Germany,* and words ending in -*ge*.
> (Exceptions: *get, geese, gear.*)

> **gi** as in *giant, giraffe, ginger, giro.* (More words, however, have a hard *g* as in *give, girl, gift, gig, giggle, gibbon, giddy.*)

> **gy** as in *gypsy, Egypt, gyroscope, gymnasium, geology, energy.*
> (Exceptions: words ending in -*ggy.*)

y as a vowel *y* acts like *i* anywhere in a word except at the beginning, as in these examples:

> **long i sound:** *my, sky, dry, why, cry, reply, try, fly, cycle, nylon, hyena, dynamite.*

> **short i sound:** *hymn, gypsy, baby, Egypt, mystery, lyric, hypnotist, dyslexic,* and all words with the suffix -*ly.*

(*y as a vowel* continues overleaf)

ir sound: *martyr, myrtle.*

ire sound: *tyre, pyre, lyre, byre, Pyrex.*

ai sound: *day, play, say, sway, crayon, Aylesbury, bayonet.*

oi sound: *boy, toy, annoy, oyster, Roy, gargoyle.*

i-e sound: *type, style, rhyme, thyme, analyse, paralyse.*

kn as in *know, knee, knife, knock, knot, knight.*

gn as in *gnat, gnome, gnaw, gnash, gnarled, gnu,* and in *reign, sign, foreign, design, campaign.*

mb as in *climb, comb, lamb, thumb, numb, bomb, tomb.*

qua **short o sound** as in *quarrel, quads, quantity, quality, quarantine, squat, squash.*

or sound as in *quarter, quartz, quart, quartet.*

(Exceptions: *square, aquarium, quark, quack, quake, earthquake.*)

wa, wo vowel sounds can be irregular after **w**, as in the following examples.

wa *was, want, wasp, wallet, wander, wash, watch, water, swallow, swat, swan.* (But: *wait, waste, wave, way, wage, wade, Wales, wax, wagon, swathe, swagger.*)

war *war, warm, warn, wart, swarm, swarthy.*

wor *work, word, worm, worse, worth, worship, world,* and *worry, worried.* (But: *wore, worn, swore, sworn, sword.*)

hard ch as in *school, Christmas, Christopher, ache, chemistry, chorus, stomach, Nicholas, chasm, chrysanthemum, chameleon, character.*

-ti + vowel a 'sh' sound as in the following examples:

> **-tion:** *station, action, fiction, auction, ignition, injection, distribution* and all other *-tion words.*

> **-tial:** *essential, confidential, initial, martial, partial.*

> **-tious:** *ambitious, fictitious, infectious, superstitious.*

> (Also: *patient, impatient, Egyptian.*)

-ci + vowel a 'sh' sound as in the following examples:

> **-cial:** *official, special, financial, racial, social.*

> **-cian:** *electrician, optician, dietician, magician, Grecian.*

> **-cious:** *gracious, spacious, precious, delicious, malicious.* (Also: *species, suspicion.*)

-si + vowel a 'sh' sound or 'zh' as in *vision, erosion, explosion, concussion, pension, mission,* and all other words ending in *-sion* and *-ssion.* Also: *Russian, Asian, Friesian, artesian.*

Associating phonic sounds with pictures
Colours

ow	1. yellow
	2. brown
marker e	white, rose, lime, jade, primrose
ee	green, coffee
ar	scarlet, mustard, carnation
oo	mushroom, maroon
oa	oatmeal
aw	tawny brown
au	auburn
ea	oatmeal
ew	pewter
ur	purple
hard g	green
soft g	ginger

Animal kingdom

ow	1. cow, owl
	2. crow, swallow
ou	mouse
or	horse
oa	goat, foal, stoat, toad
oo	kangaroo, goose
ee	sheep, chimpanzee, geese

ea *seahorse, sea lion, seal*

marker e *snake, whale, crocodile*

ir *bird*

oy *oyster, oyster catcher*

hard g *goat*

soft g *giraffe*

ph *pheasant*

Examples of phonic groups linked for spelling

Please note that the following are some examples only. The list is not meant to be exhaustive.

Long a **a** as in *acorn, baby*.

ay as in *way, play*.

ai as in *rain, aim*.

a before 'marker e' as in *gate, whale*.

ey, ei: only a few words such as *they, grey, prey, obey, survey* and *eight, weigh, weight, rein, reindeer, veil, vein, skein*.

Long e **e** as in *he, emu*.

ee as in *tree, need*.

ea as in *tea, east*.

e before 'marker e': mostly harder words, but a few met in early reading such as *these, concrete, Japanese, Chinese*.

ei: only a few words such as *receive, ceiling, seize, counterfeit*.

Appendix

Long i **i** as in *idea, tidy.*

i before 'marker e' as in *ice, hide.*

igh as in *high, sigh* and the many *-ight* words.

Also *eye.*

Long o **o** as in *open, post, no, go.*

o before 'marker e' as in *phone, home.*

oa as in *road, goal, oats.*

ow as in *grow, own, shadow.*

Also: *oh, roe, toe, woe, sew.*

Long u **u** as in *unit, usual, duty.*

u before 'marker e' as in *use, volume, nude.*

ue as in *argue, value.*

ew as in *new, few, ewe.*

Note that these letters may spell not only this 'yoo' sound, but may also spell a long 'oo' sound, as below.

Long oo sound **oo** as in *zoo, root, ooze.*

ew as in *flew, grew, jewel.*

ue as in *blue, true.*

Final t sound **t** as in *slept, kept, act.*

ed: some verbs in the past tense such as *walked, talked, jumped, bumped, smacked, smoked, picked, hoped.*

A final l
sound **ll** as in one-syllable words with a short vowel
sound like *tell, kill, doll, dull*;
also as in one-syllable words rhyming with *ball*,
like *tall, fall, Paul, haul, shawl, crawl*.

l as in one-syllable words with a long *a, e, o* or
oo sound like *tail, meal, eel, foal, pool* (but also
see *le* below);
also as in multi-syllable words with a short
final vowel sound like *total, camel, gerbil, pistol*,
and the many words ending in *-ful* such as
careful, handful (but also see *le* below).

le immediately following a long vowel as in
pale, mile, hole, rule;
also immediately following a consonant as in
bottle, apple, simple.

lle as in *gazelle, Braille* and *pipistrelle*.

(Spelling words that have a final **l** sound can
be particularly tricky. See suggestions for
helping children to learn the word 'animal',
Spelling chapter, page 144.)

A final k
sound **ck** immediately following a short vowel as in
clock, duck.

ke immediately following a long vowel as in
take, joke, except for a long *ee* sound (see below).

k immediately following a long or short *oo*
sound as in *spook, took*; immediately following
a long *ee* sound as in *speak, week*; immediately
following the sound of another consonant, as
in *think, risk*.

que: a few words such as *antique, unique, mosque*.

Index

See also the detailed Contents list, pages 5-12.

Index

Index

Index